# $100,000 and Counting

A Faith-Based Guide to Winning College Scholarships

## ASHLI MCLEAN

WESTBOW
PRESS
A DIVISION OF THOMAS NELSON

Unless otherwise noted, Scripture quotations are from the
Holman Christian Standard Version, Copyright
Used by permission. All rights reserved.
Printed in the United States

WestBow Press books may be ordered through booksellers or by contacting:

WestBow Press
A Division of Thomas Nelson
1663 Liberty Drive
Bloomington, IN 47403
www.westbowpress.com
1-(866) 928-1240

ISBN: 978-1-4497-6182-0 (sc)
ISBN: 978-1-4497-6181-3 (hc)
ISBN: 978-1-4497-6183-7 (e)

Library of Congress Control Number: 2012913885

Printed in the United States of America

WestBow Press rev. date: 08/29/2012

# Contents

# Introduction: The Proclamation

"Tuitions paid! Full ride scholarships!" The words resonated each Sunday as our congregation proclaimed by faith what we were believing God for. Every Sunday we cried out in unison: "Bills paid off, debts demolished, jobs and bonuses…" and much more. The verbiage never changed and somehow it became permanently entrenched in my spirit. The words—tuitions paid, full ride scholarships—became my battle cry. As I continued to speak those words, I knew God would hear my special request for my impending college tuition to be paid in full. I knew He could hear the faith I had when I spoke those words. There was no doubt in my mind; as my mom and I stood with the crowd and recited the proclamation each week, I knew that in the end, He **would** provide. I soon began to see that having another person—my mom—included in this faith walk with me would help spring forth my request. _**Matthew 18:19-20**_ says, _**"Again, I assure you: If two of you on earth agree about any matter that you pray for, it will done for you by My Father in heaven. For where two or three are gathered together in My name, I am there among them."**_

This book is meant to encourage you. It is meant to empower you by providing the knowledge and resources necessary to capitalize on a free college education. It is intended to motivate you to start researching the abundance of scholarship opportunities that you qualify for. I dedicate this book to the countless students and parents, particularly minorities, who feel as if they do not have access to information about scholarships. There are numerous avenues to acquire financial aid for college, and you being the wonderful and unique student that you are makes it that much greater for you. The financial aid I am referring to is not student loans, which must be repaid. Instead, I'm talking about SCHOLARSHIPS. FREE Money! I am referring to financial support that will pay for your tuition, books, fees, housing, scholastic programs, and more. And the great part is that this support will **never** have to be repaid.

My experience is a testament to the overflow of blessings that God has in store for you. I believe it is because of my faith and diligence that He has provided me with the finances to graduate from Hampton University with having accumulated over $100,000 in scholarships. In doing so, He has also given me the platform or "lampstand" to share my story, tips, and resources with others so that they may benefit from the information. <u>**Matthew 5:15-16**</u> *says:* **"No one lights a lamp and puts it under a basket, but rather on a lampstand, and it gives light for all who are in the house. In the same way, your light must shine before men, so that they may see your good works and give glory to your Father in heaven."**

It is my hope that you take full advantage of the information presented in this book as it provides you with a compilation of my experiences, advice, resources, and scriptural references to help you on this journey. I have included valuable insight and tips from those who are more attuned to the avenues of obtaining scholarships, including guidance counselors and community foundation representatives. This book offers their perspectives and wealth of knowledge.

So let's begin this journey. It is your turn to receive your blessing! I will continue to encourage you throughout this book because I believe our Father has so much more in store for you than you could ever imagine.

# 1

# A WINNER'S MINDSET

"Why apply? I'll never get it." "This process is too complicated and too time consuming." "I won't get this scholarship; there are too many people applying for it." "Why apply? It's only $250. It's not like it's $2,500." **STOP!** How many times have you whispered these thoughts to yourself? There are so many reasons you can give as to why you shouldn't apply for scholarships. However, many opportunities are lost because students automatically assume they won't receive any money. Defeat—*or VICTORY*—begins in the mind! This is the absolute first step in accessing that free college money: Develop a winner's mindset. You **CAN** win scholarships. Know that you will receive. Know that it is possible for you to win a $1,000 scholarship, or even a $100,000 scholarship. And how do you do that? By faith. **Hebrews 11:1** says: **"Now faith is the assurance of what is hoped for, the proof of what is not seen."** You may not see it, but you know it is there. I began my freshman year of college with neither a full-ride scholarship nor multiple scholarships to cover my four-year cost of attendance. However, I somehow **KNEW** that I would walk away with my tuition fully paid for prior to graduation. I prayed that God would provide scholarships for me. I proclaimed it. I spoke life to it. It was my faith that opened the door for me to receive abundantly, and it will be the same for you. The Word says, **"Consider it a great joy, my brothers, whenever you experience various trials, knowing that the testing of your faith produces endurance** ["endurance" is "perseverance" in other versions]**"** (**James 1:2-3**). It further states in **verses 6** and **7**, **"But let him ask in faith without doubting. For the doubter is like the surging sea, driven and tossed**

***by the wind. That person should not expect to receive anything from the LORD."*** Do not be consumed by the trials you are experiencing in trying to obtain scholarship money. It's just a test. Having faith that God will provide this for you will build up your perseverance and patience. It will strengthen your endurance to seek out scholarships and it will lead you to the right resources. Subsequently, the strengthening of your faith will produce an overwhelming confidence in you that you didn't know you possessed. In time you will begin to have an assurance that, without a shadow of doubt, God will provide. Your confidence will increase your expectation that says, "God will help me". When you are walking in obedience by listening to Him and following His commands, and you are in line with His will, all you'll have to do is wait silently on Him in <u>expectation</u>. Pray for what you desire, have faith, and it shall be done.

I'd like to share a story. Three months before my college graduation, I won a $7,500 scholarship. I was ecstatic because this would cover all but $786 that I still owed to Hampton University. That burden would be off of my back well before walking across the stage. My degree program was a five-year, joint degree program in which I received both my bachelor's and master's degrees. By this time, I was finishing my master's degree coursework. The two years prior had proved to be the hardest I had ever worked in my educational career and all I wanted to do was graduate on time and with minimal debt. Not too long after receiving news of the scholarship, however, I was sent an email from the scholarship committee stating that because I was a graduate student, the scholarship would have to be rescinded. Talk about being angry and hurt! Not once on the scholarship application was a classification requirement listed. In fact, the classification requirement was listed as "open" and this particular scholarship organization provided numerous awards for both undergraduate and graduate students, so I initially did not see my graduate status as a problem. I could not understand why the scholarship would be taken back. I even found the same scholarship listed on two other websites. Both sites also showed that there was no specific classification requirement. I presented these facts to the organization. I argued my case as best as I could, but I got nowhere. The scholarship was retracted.

I remember releasing my frustrations to my mom. I told her how unfair it was. Seventy-five hundred dollars is by no means a small amount of money to be "playing with", especially with graduation quickly approaching. But after I let it all go, I calmly, yet boldly, told her, "It's okay. God will provide another $7,500 scholarship—in that exact amount." She looked at me a bit perplexed, but I knew He would because this situation was not a coincidence; it was God's hand at work. I already knew before I won the scholarship that He would provide for my financial needs, and my mindset did not change when the scholarship was revoked. I merely had to look back over the past four years to see how, time and time again, God provided scholarship dollars for me—many times at the last minute. I saw firsthand that He may not have been early, but He was never late. If God had already promised this to me, then what I was dealing with was only a test of my faith. I was overwhelmed with a confidence I could not explain, and an expectation of Him to provide.

> "Blessed is the man who trusts in the LORD,
> whose confidence indeed is the LORD.
> He will be like a tree planted by water:
> it sends its root out toward a stream,
> it doesn't fear when heat comes,
> and its foliage remains green.
> It will not worry in a year of drought
> or cease producing fruit." (Jeremiah 17:7-8)

You'll come to find that because you trust Him, His favor will be on your life. He will reward you for putting your faith in Him. I was confident the $7,500 would be supplied in time.

Shortly thereafter, I received an email stating that the director of that organization was able to secure a $5,000 scholarship for me in lieu of the previous one. Whew! Only twenty-five hundred dollars left to get. The director stated that she would try to access the other $2,500 for me. With one month to go and constant communication with the director, I had not received the remaining $2,500 to pay off my student account balance. For two weeks I pleaded with God, "God, You said You would provide. I know this is what You have for me but God, where is this other $2,500 going to come from? I have less than one month until graduation. I need you to show up, even if it's in the midnight hour." With 11 days to go until graduation, I got the email I had been waiting for! Not only had the director found another $2,500 for me, but she also stated that the check was already being processed and she would call me once it cleared.

What do you say to that?! Is God amazing or what? Imagine if I had doubted. Imagine if the testing of my faith in earlier years had not produced perseverance and expectation. Surely this would not be my testimony now. It is your faith that God wants to see. I once heard someone say, "God is not moved by your self-pity; He is moved by your faith." He wants to know that even in the midst of your struggles, even in the midnight hour, you will trust Him wholeheartedly and expectantly to do just what He promised. **_Psalm 62:5_** says, **_"Rest in God alone, for my hope_** ["hope" is "expectation" in other versions] **_comes from Him"._** "Expectation" is described as anticipation, looking forward to, belief, and prospect. With God, know that you can stop struggling, resisting, and coercing for what you want. Simply do as He instructs, keep your focus and praise on Him, and wait expectantly. He <u>will</u> pull through for you.

Understand that scholarship money is not just given away at your high school or college—it is everywhere! Churches, local community organizations, and even your parents' employers provide scholarships. Also, scholarships are not for the selected few. Millions of scholarship dollars are available for anyone and everyone who is willing to pursue these opportunities, especially those who are of a minority background or come from low-income households. There is a scholarship out there for every student. Even if you already have a scholarship that fully covers your college tuition and/or room and board, you can still obtain additional scholarships that will pay for your textbooks, supplies, and miscellaneous expenses. Case in point: Amtrak offers a scholarship that pays for your travel expenses to any destination (applies only to traveling on Amtrak trains, of course). This means free transportation home during college breaks or to wherever your spring break plans may take you.

According to the College Board's "Trends in College Pricing," the 2011-2012 average total cost of tuition, fees, room and board at:

- An in-state public institution was $17,131 or $68,524 total for four years;

- A public, out-of-state institution was $29,657 or $118,628 total for four years; and
- A private, nonprofit institution was $38,589 or $154,356 total for four years.

The report assumes an additional $4,296 yearly for textbooks, supplies, transportation and other expenses.[1] My four-year education at Hampton University, a private college, cost $103,668. None of these figures are imaginary; they are approximately what you can expect to pay for a college education today. Because of this, it is important that you understand how to attain as much scholarship money as you can. Do not doubt your ability to receive scholarships. Rather, believe that the effort and diligence you put into applying for them will pay off. You can't receive what you don't apply for. Have faith that you won't simply receive one scholarship, but that you'll receive many!

*"I always go into a race understanding that, yes, I can lose, but I can also win. One of my philosophies is 'if somebody has to win, why not me?'"*
*—Mark Crear, two-time Olympic medalist*

# 2

# WHAT IS A SCHOLARSHIP AND WHAT OTHER NON-DEBT SOURCES OF FINANCIAL AID ARE AVAILABLE?

Financial aid is funding given to a student to help pay for educational expenses in college. Such expenses include tuition (the cost of classes), class fees, room and board (dorm and meal plans), books, supplies, and miscellaneous fees. Prospective students receive a "financial aid package" from every college they are accepted to. This package encompasses debt and non-debt sources. Debt sources are those which have to be repaid. The most common form of debt sources are student loans, which may be provided by the college, the government, or external resources like Sallie Mae. Non-debt sources are funding that do not have to be repaid. Such sources are what this book focuses on, particularly scholarships. Non-debt sources include scholarships, grants, and work study programs.

By definition, a scholarship is money granted to a student for higher education purposes. The most common type of scholarship is a merit scholarship. This type rewards a student for his/her academics, athletic abilities, or extracurricular talents. Regardless of the income level of the student's household, he/she can receive this scholarship based on those aforementioned merits. The most important criterion in receiving this type of scholarship is usually the student's academics: grades and SAT/ACT scores. At the graduate level, scholarships are often referred to as fellowships. There are also need-based scholarships. The criteria for receiving these types of scholarships are based on the financial situation of the student's family. The scholarship organization will evaluate the student's true "need" for the scholarship to obtain a college education by using a measurement tool known as the Free Application for Federal Student Aid (FAFSA). The FAFSA is sponsored through the government and will be discussed later in the book. Other types of scholarships include those that are provided based on students' characteristics or attributes (i.e. race, disabilities), as well as intended college major and career interests.

Another non-debt source of financial aid is a grant. Grants are usually provided by the government, nonprofit organizations, and community foundations. These funds are generally given to students for a more specified use than that of scholarships. This may include project research, overseas study programs, or even starting one's own business while in school. The most common of these is the Federal Pell Grant. Sponsored by the government, it provides need-based money to low-income undergraduate students and certain post-baccalaureate students. Grant amounts are normally dependent on the following: the student's financial need, as determined by his/her Expected Family Contribution (EFC) on the FAFSA; the cost of attendance at the intended college; the student's enrollment status (full-time or part-time); and whether the student attends for a full academic year or less. Students may use their grants at any one of approximately 5,400 participating postsecondary institutions. The maximum Pell grant award for the 2011-2012 school year was $5,500.

A final source of financial aid that does not have to be repaid is work study. Work study programs allow students to work part-time jobs on campus in return for financial assistance. The Federal Work-Study (FWS) Program is sponsored by the government and allows the Department of Education to provide funding for the program to over 3,400 participating colleges and universities. Each school's financial aid department determines the amount of FWS awards to provide to students. At the graduate level, students can obtain a graduate assistantship. This form of work study is also used in a part-time capacity on campus or, more commonly, to perform major-related work such as serving as a teaching assistant or doing research for a thesis. Essentially, work study is a student "working off" the cost of his/her education.

Don't worry about your ability to seize scholarships and these other non-debt resources for college. Because you are faithful, God will provide. **_Luke 12:24-26_** *tells us,* **"Consider the ravens: they don't sow or reap; they don't have a storeroom or a barn; yet God feeds them. Aren't you worth much more than the birds? Can any of you add a cubit to his height** ["a cubit to his height" is "add one moment to his lifespan" in other versions] **by worrying? If then you're not able to do even a little thing, why worry about the rest?"** There is no point in worrying since God already knows what you need and desire. He wants you to come to Him with your petitions, in full faith that He will provide. Once you do that, apply for all the scholarships that come your way and simply watch Him work.

# 3

# WHY YOU NEED TO APPLY FOR SCHOLARSHIPS (BESIDES THE FACT THAT IT'S FREE MONEY!)

Obtaining free money for your college education should be all the motivation you need to apply for scholarships. The stress of having to take out loans or to put your family in a financial bind in order for you to go to college is alleviated. If this isn't enough encouragement for you, then consider these six other benefits that can come with winning scholarships:

1. **You get invited to fun events sponsored by the hosting organization.** Galas, parties, and other exciting events may be an added benefit for you as a recipient of a scholarship. During my senior year in high school, I won a scholarship from the Virginia Scholarship and Youth Development Fund (VSYDF). In addition to the scholarship, I was invited to attend its annual gala and to become involved in "The Tim Reid Celebrity Weekend" which usually includes: a celebrity basketball game; a charity golf tournament; a health awareness fair at a local university; and a social evening mixer at a lounge. As the founder of the VSYDF, Tim Reid—most known for his role as Ray Campbell on the hit television series "Sister, Sister"—invites his Hollywood friends out every year to the weekend celebration in an effort to raise awareness for the

foundation and to attract potential donors to help fund students' college educations. Celebrities who have partaken in the weekend events over the last few years include Will Smith, Tatyana Ali, Kyla Pratt, and T'onex, among many others. As a recipient, I was able to interact with such celebrities and build relationships that will prove invaluable as the years progress.

2. **You are provided opportunities to speak on behalf of how the scholarship has helped you.** Many times, scholarship recipients are invited to events like those mentioned above to share with others how the scholarship has helped meet their educational expenses and achieve their dreams, thereby encouraging potential donors to also contribute to the organization. Whether I was asked to do this or not, whether I did so in a formal or informal manner, I never hesitated in telling others what receiving those scholarships has meant to me. Doing so has opened up many other opportunities for me to 'pay it forward', such as helping others receive scholarships, pursue a college education, and achieve their dreams as well. I've realized that it is not only my obligation to help others, but that I also look forward to finding ways of supporting other college hopefuls.

3. **You get to meet important and influential leaders.** Of course, meeting celebrities at the organization's events is always fun. But meeting people who can assist you in moving to the next level of where you want to go with your career once you graduate is even better. A great example is the experience I received when I won a scholarship from the Executive Leadership Council (ELC). Comprised of over 500 of the most senior African-American corporate executives of America's Fortune 500 companies, the ELC focuses on "building an inclusive business leadership pipeline, developing African-American corporate leaders—one student and one executive at a time."[2] As a scholarship recipient, I was invited to its week-long symposium. I received an amazing, all-expenses-paid trip to Manhattan for the symposium that included: company visits to meet with some of the nation's most powerful and influential African-American executives, including Ken Chenault, Chief

Executive Officer (CEO) of American Express and one of only six African-American CEOs of today's Fortune 500 companies; having access to internships on the spot; gaining premier career advice from seasoned and expert executives; and networking to establish solid relationships with people from a plethora of industries. It was even at this gala where I interacted with the President of the business division at Prudential that I work in today. As a business student with an intended career in corporate America, I could not have asked for a more amazing opportunity. I had access to all of this because I wrote one essay! The Jackie Robinson Foundation and the National Urban League's Black Executive Exchange Program (BEEP) are other great examples of being able to interact with important and influential leaders as a scholarship recipient.

4. **You get acknowledged before your superiors and your peers.**
It is an awesome feeling when the hard work you put into attaining a scholarship pays off through recognition. To have those around you acknowledge your diligence and be able to celebrate your achievement with you is as much a reward as the scholarship itself. During my senior year at Hampton, I received the President's Award. As the winner, I was acknowledged at the Senior Banquet before the senior class, university faculty, and Hampton University's President Dr. William Harvey. This was a total surprise; I had no idea beforehand that I had won the scholarship nor that I would be recognized in such an open forum. I was unable to attend the event, but to have my professors and classmates approach me the next day to congratulate me was a special moment of my college tenure.

5. **Instant publicity!** Many organizations will use you as a symbol of the good work they are doing in supporting the education of students. You may be featured on local radio stations and in company newsletters and websites. A great example of this is when I received a scholarship from a local gospel radio station, Star 94.1FM in Hampton, VA. Each week, the station selected one outstanding student of the area's seven cities. As a winner, I received a savings bond. The station also broadcasted a blurb about me and my achievements, which was announced daily to an audience of

over one million people in the seven-city, Hampton Roads area of Virginia.

6.  **The scholarship may award you annually.** Many scholarships provide funding to recipients for four to five years of college tenure. As a recipient of the VSYDF, I was able to receive the same scholarship amount for up to ten semesters—five years of college! The same goes for The Beazley Foundation scholarship I received as a business student at Hampton.

Now having looked at these other motivation factors, let's jump right into the guidelines you need to follow to win scholarships!

# 4

# GUIDING PRINCIPLES

I have eight guiding principles that I encourage you to follow to obtain as much scholarship money as possible. All of these I personally took action upon. I share with you my own experiences, as well as those of my colleagues. I also give you invaluable advice from people who know the college and scholarship processes best. So let's get started!

## Principle #1: Start Early!

The first day of your senior year of high school, you should be banging on your guidance counselors' door, inquiring about scholarships. You should be researching scholarships online. You should be asking friends, family, co-workers, your church, and associations you're linked with about scholarships they provide or know of.

The beginning of senior year is the earliest I would advise you to start actively seeking and applying for scholarships. The majority of college scholarships are awarded to high school seniors and current college students. This is logical, of course, because the hosting organizations need proof that you have been accepted to a college and that you indeed plan to attend. Searching and applying for scholarships is a time-consuming endeavor. It takes much due diligence. Therefore, becoming fully committed at the beginning of your senior year is highly recommended. Although I personally never encountered scholarships that I could apply for before my senior year, it doesn't hurt for you to engage with your counselor to determine if any are available. In fact, you could use the end of your junior year or the summer before your senior year to start researching and writing essays for scholarships that you qualify for so that by the time your senior year rolls around you aren't spending too much time and effort doing this. If scholarship opportunities present themselves to you, do not hesitate to take advantage of them! For example, you could easily secure the National Merit Scholarship based on your scores of the Preliminary SAT (PSAT), which is taken during your junior year. High school juniors and younger usually win money for college via essay competitions.

> _What the Guidance Counselor Says:_ "_Obtaining a scholarship even before entering high school is possible. There are many scholarship competitions that take place for students as early as 6th grade. Art competitions are one such example. Also, essay competitions are available for both junior high and high school students from sites like Fastweb and College Board._"

Another key component of starting early is to complete the Free Application for Federal Student Aid (FAFSA) as early as possible beginning January 1. This January 1st date is applicable during both your senior year of high school and every year of your college matriculation. The FAFSA determines the amount of financial assistance the government will provide to you based on your family's income, savings and contributions to your education, and your personal savings for college. Do not wait until the tax season deadline (April 15) is right around the corner to submit it. The earlier you submit your FAFSA, the more financial aid the government can supply you with. The government has a priority deadline of February 15 for FAFSA filings. All FAFSAs that are submitted by this date are privy to the federal funds and FAFSA information that the government releases on March 15 to colleges and universities across the nation. If you submit your FAFSA much later than February 15, you run the risk of receiving less money in your financial aid package since by that time the colleges have already issued a great portion of what came from the government to students who met the priority deadline. So even if you have to estimate as best as possible the figures that are requested on the FAFSA, do so.

If you are already in college, understand that is never too late to start applying for scholarships. Start researching, asking professors, and applying every school year from now until you graduate. You must be committed and dedicated if you want the money. Once you start, do not stop, even in times of not winning. Keep pressing, and you will reap what you sow! Do not apply for scholarships simply because you think you may win a few; apply for scholarships because you *know* you will win every single one for which you submit an application and/or essay. It is a mindset. It is a showing of your faith. It is a confidence exuded from your faith. You prayed for it, so why not believe that you have already received it?

> *"Jesus replied to them, 'Have faith in God. I assure you: If anyone says to this mountain, 'Be lifted and thrown up into the sea,' and does not doubt in his heart but believes that what he says will happen, it will be done for him. Therefore I tell you, all the things you pray and ask for—believe that you have received them, and you will have them."*
> **(Mark 11:22-24)**

## Principle #2: Utilize These Resources.

A) ***Guidance Counselors, Scholarship Coordinators, and Financial Aid Officers.*** The approach in accessing and winning scholarships is to start locally, then branch out to national scholarships. Why? Because your most lucrative scholarship resource is also your most local resource. Your #1 resource in searching for, applying for, and winning scholarships is your high school guidance counselor. Let me repeat: <u>YOUR #1 RESOURCE IS YOUR GUIDANCE COUNSELOR</u>! He/she should be your best friend during your senior year. This person is a walking wealth of knowledge. Your guidance counselor is the liaison between you (the student) and the many organizations that offer scholarships to your school. These organizations go directly to the guidance counselors to advertise and disseminate their scholarship information. This is done by mailing or emailing information about scholarships they are offering to every local high school, bringing the scholarship packets to the schools, and sometimes even expecting the guidance counselors to do the advertising if it is the same scholarship offered each year. In addition, some organizations work with the guidance counselors to draft the scholarship application! Thus, your counselor is always aware of what scholarships are available on a continual basis as well as what you qualify for. In fact, some counselors are now allowing students and parents to sign up for email lists that automatically send scholarship updates. Take advantage of such opportunities!

My first year's college expenses were approximately $24,000. Nearly all of this was covered with scholarships I won directly from the support, direction and commitment of my guidance counselor. His work ethic ensured that I received scholarships not only from local organizations, business, and churches, but also money I was entitled to from my chosen college and in-state assistance. Thus, your best bet is to start with your guidance counselor. It's also a good idea to build a relationship with your counselor because he/she serves as a mentor. Guidance counselors help students navigate through the college and scholarship processes, which may seem a bit overwhelming and discouraging at first. There will be times when you need someone to give you that extra push to meet a scholarship application deadline. They will certainly be there to push you.

Most scholarships do not flood your counselor's office at the beginning of the school year; they are provided and updated on a continual basis. You may go to your counselor's office on Monday to find a particular scholarship available, and then by Friday that same organization may have submitted another scholarship that you also qualify for. High school guidance counselors are also very aware of scholarships that are available to students who plan to attend universities in-state. Much of that same information is relayed to the state high schools by the universities themselves, the government, or by colleagues (i.e. other guidance counselors). Hence, it is important to befriend such a resource. He/she is the key to winning scholarships early on.

For those of you who have graduated from high school and are already in college, the guideline of starting early applies to you as well. It is imperative that you get to know your scholarship coordinator and/or financial aid officer as soon as possible. Establish a solid relationship with that person, or both if they are two different people. They should know you by name and you should be in their offices frequently to find out about new scholarship opportunities and other avenues of paying for school without taking out student loans. Just like high school counselors, these individuals are aware of thousands of dollars in free money waiting to be applied for by students of the university. And even better, they are privy to much more information and financial aid that counselors at the high school level aren't, including those non-debt sources mentioned earlier (work-study, graduate assistantships, fellowships, and grants). This is primarily because they have a close relationship with the departments throughout the university, many of which provide such resources to their students. It is also because these scholarship coordinators and financial aid officers have a more direct access to government-funded money and national organizations that provide scholarships to students of universities across the nation.

Your counselor can only do so much in attempting to inform students of available scholarships. It is up to YOU to seek out that free money. Particularly at the college level, professors and counselors will be the first to tell you that too many scholarships go unapplied. In light of this, you must aggressively seek out these opportunities to guarantee your success in competing with other students. You are guaranteed to win more scholarships by actively seeking them than by not doing so.

Be sure to also leverage your faculty as a resource. Oftentimes they have ties to the educational community which keeps them abreast of scholarship opportunities for their students. They are aware of additional, unadvertised scholarships for which you may be eligible. All it takes is for you to ask. My 11th grade U.S. History teacher, for example, was the scholarship coordinator at my high school for a particular local scholarship. Although I found out about this after graduation, me simply inquiring to her about scholarships could've provided me with more money for college.

> _What the Guidance Counselor Says:_ "_Take the time to develop relationships with your teachers. It may prove more beneficial than simply accessing scholarship information. I once knew a student who submitted a letter of recommendation from his 2nd grade teacher for a scholarship. His application automatically stood out from others. The fact that he had such a good rapport with a teacher from nearly 10 years prior said a lot._"

Although I was an active seeker of scholarships, the greatest scholarship opportunities seemed to have found their way to me. For example, on many occasions I noticed scholarships posted on a bulletin board outside my Dean's office in the School of Business for weeks at a time, many of which were never applied to by students. On three different occasions, I won scholarships by applying to the listings on that board. The first was a $5,000 scholarship. The second was $10,000. The third was $1,000. Before applying for each one I remember thinking, "Man, this scholarship has been up here for a while." And it was precisely at that moment that I would be compelled to apply. It certainly wasn't me. I've always been a go-getter; however, I would see those listings for weeks and not apply. Then suddenly, an inexplicable optimism would come over me, hinting that I should apply. I call that God. I call it His plan. The point is, these scholarships were listed for the entire School of Business student body to see (as well as for students of other majors who roamed the halls). For weeks, thousands of students could've applied, yet I consistently got the feeling that I was the only one who actually did so. It was in those moments that I chose to listen to God's quiet encouragement, and to act on it. More than once did that decision pay off.

Students do not receive scholarships because they do not apply. It's as simple as that. You have already lost out on free money when you ***choose*** not to apply. Utilize the knowledge and insight of your counselors, coordinators and officers, and start applying! You'll come to find out that you are only one of a handful (if even that) applying.

B) ***Family and Friends.*** Surround yourself with like-minded people! Build your support system with friends and family members who are actively seeking out scholarships or who can help you in your scholarship search. If your friends and family are not doing this currently, get them involved! Let them know that you need their support. Parents, in particular, are more apt to respond to this request than friends because the expense of obtaining a college education typically falls on your family. Many parents may not even think to search for scholarships until you ask them to do so. It's all about building your support system.

Let's say you have three close friends whom you ask to support you, and only one of them is able to find scholarships for you. The other two, instead, forwarded your request to their parents, who ended up finding some scholarships that you qualify for from their co-workers, friends, and other acquaintances. Now your initial support system of three friends has grown much larger. The knowledge base of scholarships you have just inherited is invaluable.

Likewise, getting your parents involved can be beneficial. My mom was just as persistent in seeking out scholarships for me as I was for myself. She made sure that I was aware of various scholarships and that I was actually applying for them. She even made sure that I sent a thank you note to some of those organizations, whether or not I won! Having her oversight and persistence in my life kept me focused on my goal of going to school debt-free. Therefore, do not underestimate the effort, knowledge, or resource of your parents once you ask them to help you in your scholarship search.

Aside from enlisting your parents to search for scholarships, recognize that they may have access to scholarship information through the many networks they are in, including their workplaces. Many companies have their own foundations that provide scholarships to children of employees. Be sure to research online and have your parents ask if their employers offer scholarships for both the general population and children of employees. If your parents work for the government, for example, the Federal Employee Emergency Assistance (FEEA) is an organization that you want to become very familiar with. The Verizon Foundation's Verizon Scholarship Program and the YUM! Andy Pearson Scholarship Program are also well-known scholarship programs for children of employees. Other companies that provide scholarships dollars to employees' dependents include: Walmart, Bank of America, Ford, Lowe's, State Farm, Wachovia, Wells Fargo, UPS, PepsiCo, Intel, Macy's, Humana, Sunoco, and Michelin, among many others.

C) *Corporations.* Corporate philanthropy is its own operational division within many of today's top companies. They have foundations that are dedicated solely to supporting their communities by engaging in activities like providing scholarship dollars to students. You can go directly to their websites to find scholarships they offer. Big-name companies like Walmart, ExxonMobil, Coca-Cola, and AT&T have renowned scholarship programs. These and other Fortune 500 companies provide millions of dollars in scholarships each year and many of them have separate, additional scholarship programs for minority students. For example, Boeing specifically provides scholarships to undergraduate students who attend Historically Black Colleges & Universities (HBCUs; institutions with an educational and student life experience tailored to serve African American students) that the company is partnered with. Vanguard hosts its Minority Scholarship Program to students entering their junior and senior years of college. The scholarship provides up to $10,000 to minority students pursuing business, economics, finance, or accounting. United Health Group provides scholarships for diverse students through third-party foundations, such as the Tom Joyner Foundation, in an attempt to increase the number of diverse professionals working in the healthcare industry.

In addition to providing its own minority scholarship, General Motors distributes scholarship money through third-party providers such as the National Action Council for Minorities in Engineering (NACME). The United Negro College Fund (UNCF) is also a major partner with corporations wishing to distribute scholarships to minority students. For example, the Hershey's Scholarship Program awards $5,000 to rising and current college freshmen with at least a 2.5 GPA. To be eligible, applicants must also attend a UNCF member college or one of the Pennsylvania colleges listed on that particular scholarship's information page on the UNCF website. Pfizer and Verizon also offer scholarships through the UNCF website. Take advantage of the money these corporations and their third-party partners are offering!

**D)** ***Credit Unions and Commercial Banks.*** Like corporations, credit unions and banks have wealth that they are not shy of sharing as part of their philanthropic mission. Visit your local credit unions and banks and inquire about scholarships they offer. Most agencies require you to be a member in order to be eligible for the scholarship. Summit Credit Union is an example. Serving the Madison, WI areas, Summit offers a yearly, $1,500 scholarship to five high school students who are members. This past year, applicants were required to write an essay explaining the differences between credit unions and banks. How easy is that?! Virginia Credit Union offers scholarships to members who are entering their freshmen, sophomore, junior, or senior years and are taking at least 9 credit hours per semester. The Richmond Chapter of Credit Union Scholarship, however, serving the Richmond, VA area, does not even mandate you to be a member in order to qualify as long as one of your parents is a member.

SunTrust offers its yearly Off to College Scholarship Sweepstakes. It is open to high school seniors and current college students. Membership, financial need, and grade point average are not even factors. So if you have a 2.1 GPA or your parents have already saved and documented $30,000 for your college education, you still have the same chances of winning as the student who has a 3.9 GPA and comes from a low-income household. A winner is selected every two weeks from October to May (15 winners total) and the prize is a $1,000 scholarship. All you have to do is fill out an entry form on the SunTrust website. US Bank offers the US Bank Online Scholarship which gives out 40 awards in the amount of $1,000 every year to high school seniors and college undergraduates.

E) **Church.** You don't have to study theology in order to secure a scholarship from your church. Countless churches offer scholarships to their graduating high school seniors and current college students. A great example is Cascade United Methodist Church in Atlanta, GA. Under the church's Higher Education Ministry, it is sponsoring over 90 different scholarships, grants and book awards for the 2012-2013 school year[3]. Of these, nearly half will be awarded to students who are not members of the church! If your local house of worship does not provide scholarships, then check within your denomination at the national level.

F) **School Organizations.** School clubs and organizations are great extracurricular activities for you to get involved with in high school and in college. Participate in those activities that cater to your interests, hobbies, and career aspirations. They provide a fun way of interacting with fellow students and trying new things. More beneficial, they provide scholarships for members. This is especially true for national clubs. For example, the Future Business Leaders of America (FBLA), the Family, Career and Community Leaders of America (FCCLA), the National Beta Club, the Health Occupations Students of America (HOSA), and the Technology Student Association (TSA) are a few common high school clubs that offer scholarships to its members. The same holds true at the collegiate level. The National Black MBA Association, for instance, provides a $5,000 scholarship to presidents of its collegiate chapters.

As an added benefit, extracurricular clubs and organizations provide opportunities for its members to participate in national competitions and conferences to win scholarships and gain exposure. While in college my friend DeQuan, a graduate of Virginia State University, became a member of the National Society of Minorities in Hospitality (NSMH). He participated in its essay competition about how the hospitality industry could improve its sustainability efforts. He won a $3,000 scholarship. When I asked him about the exposure it provided him, he said, "The experience made me who I am today. Since I wrote that piece, I was respected and invited to speak with several important leaders in the industry who then gave me chances to improve initiatives in organizations such as Marriott & IHG Corporation."

During my junior and senior years in high school, I participated in the marching band. The Band Boosters was the parent-run, support organization of the band. It helped us fundraise for trips and other expenses, as well as provided us with logistical and parental support during our many band competitions. Not only was I able to travel to Alabama to compete in the National High School High-Stepping Marching Band Competition (and win!), but I was also able to secure more scholarship money. With extra funds left over at the end of the year, the Band Boosters was able to provide scholarships for each graduating senior.

As a musician, you can easily secure a scholarship to play in your chosen university's Marching Band, Concert Band, Orchestra, or the like. I have friends who received full-tuition scholarships to do just that.

As a college student, you are sure to be tempted into joining a fraternity or sorority. Not only are they known for their crazy parties and invaluable networks for post-college career opportunities, but they are also known for generously providing scholarships. All of the "Divine Nine" of black colleges (Alpha Kappa Alpha, Zeta Phi Beta, Alpha Phi Alpha, etc.), for example, offer scholarships to entering and current college students in some capacity. And many times, the recipient doesn't have to be a member or even intend to become a member. You can also access scholarships from alumni chapters of fraternities and sororities in your community, as well as at the national level. Get out and talk to people who are involved in these organizations as members or friends and family of members. Start with your family, then your church, and branch off from there. You'd be surprised at the wealth of resources you have in the people around you.

G) **Interests & Hobbies (outside of school clubs).** Even your interests outside of school can be utilized for college scholarships. What are some things you like to do in your free time? What do you find yourself doing quite often that you truly enjoy? For me, it's playing basketball. I've been playing since the age of 7. I played in local leagues and in high school, but I was never a "star athlete". I just love the game. Even in my free time today I round up my friends to get a game or two going. Two summers ago, I came across a scholarship jointly sponsored by Converse and Sports 790 The Zone, a sports radio station in Atlanta. The scholarship selected a winner every month and required the applicant to write a short essay on why he/she loves basketball. Talk about the perfect type of subject for me to write about! I put my heart into that essay as I am very passionate about the game. And I won. What I love most about this scholarship is that I was required to put the money into a college savings plan account through the state of Georgia's 529 Program. By the time I withdrew the money to pay for educational expenses, the dollar amount was more than what I had initially put in due to interest accrual.

How about chess? Are you good at it? Many colleges offer scholarships to students who compete in and win various chess tournaments. Take a look at the University of Maryland at Baltimore County. The school provides a full tuition, room and board scholarship to a chess player, depending on qualification and competition. Some of your more serious, professional-type hobbies can also get you into college without having to pay anything. For example, your years spent taking dance lessons may pay off by you receiving a full-tuition scholarship to a collegiate dance academy like The Julliard School. Or say you are a stellar athlete: gymnastics, football, golf, basketball, track and field, wrestling, baseball, swimming and diving—you name it, and I guarantee there is a scholarship out there for you to compete in at the collegiate level. Of course, you will still have to maintain good grades in order to be eligible to play for the NCAA, the governing association of the majority of our nation's intercollegiate athletics. If playing a sport is your intended method of paying for college, start early by involving yourself in an associated organization that will provide you with more exposure, such as the Amateur Athletic Union (AAU), Pop Warner, or other various seasonal and community leagues and tournaments.

Even the YMCA offers scholarships on a city-by-city basis. If you are a member at your local Y, inquire about scholarships that are offered. The YMCA of Boston, Dallas, and Ocala are a few branches that offer scholarships to local members. If your YMCA does not offer scholarships, then check with other YMCAs in surrounding cities. If fitness is particularly something that you are passionate about, then apply for United Youth Fitness's $1,500 scholarship. All you have to do is submit an essay on what fitness means to you. Or maybe you are deeply involved in community work. Lowe's is awarding $2,500 to 140 students for the 2012-2013 school year to students based on their community service work. Ultimately, hobbies in which you dedicate years to have the ability to provide you with a source of financial assistance for college.

**H)** *Community Service.* Link yourself up with organizations that provide scholarship dollars for your efforts in the community. Whether you volunteer for one hour a few times a year or for three hours every week, the time you dedicate to volunteering will open the door for free money for college. The Disabled American Veterans organization, for example, hosts the Jesse Brown Memorial Youth Scholarship. The scholarship is awarded to young volunteers who give their time at local Veterans Affairs (VA) medical centers. Since 2000, the scholarship program has awarded 123 scholarships worth $450,066.[4] The Samuel Huntington Public Service award is another. Although harder to win, as only one person is awarded annually, the award provides a $10,000 stipend for a graduating college senior to pursue one year of public service anywhere in the world. To apply, students must develop a proposal that encompasses any activity that furthers the public good.

Kohl's sponsors a scholarship program that is based solely on community service. The Kohl's Cares Scholarship Program rewards over 2,000 students aged 6 to 18 with over $400,000 worth of scholarship money dependent on detailed and documented volunteer efforts. Regional winners are awarded $1,000; national winners are awarded $10,000 along with Kohl's commitment to donate $1,000 to a nonprofit organization on each winner's behalf.[5] A well-known, community-focused organization is Rotary International. Its Ambassadorial Scholarships send undergraduate and graduate students to study abroad while supporting Rotary's mission to advance world understanding, goodwill, and peace. Kiwanis International is a similar organization. Scholarships vary by chapter. So get out there, stay active in your community, and receive scholarship money in return!

I) **Case Competitions, Science Challenges, and other Scholarship Competitions.** During my last year at Hampton University, I entered the Prudential Financial Business Case Competition. Prudential heavily recruits at Hampton, and each year it sponsors this competition exclusively for Hampton students for the purpose of attracting and hiring minority interns and full-time employees. The case presents a real-world challenge for the company and students form teams to compete with each other for the best solution. The top three teams are flown to the company headquarters in New Jersey to present their solutions to a panel of judges that include some of the most senior executives of the company. The teams are ranked, and students of all three teams walk away with a prize, with first place receiving a cash prize. My team won first place for the 2011 competition, and each member took home a $7,000 check.

There are many types of competitions that provide students with scholarships or cash for college. The Siemens Foundation has a renowned competition for high school students interested in science, math, and technology. Students can participate as individuals or as part of a team. The competition requires students to undertake scientific research projects, either projects taken on outside of school or those that are currently being worked on for a class assignment. Winners receive scholarships ranging from $1,000 to $100,000 for both individuals and teams. Scholarships awarded are sent directly to the selected university.

Intel hosts its yearly Science Talent Search. It is similar to the Siemens Competition in that high school students submit projects to be judged for scholarship dollars. The top 40 finalists win scholarships from a pool of $1.25 million. The first-place winner receives a four-year, $100,000 scholarship; second place wins a $75,000 scholarship; third place, $50,000, and so on. In addition, each finalist receives an all-expense paid trip to Washington D.C. to meet government officials including either the President or Vice President of the United States, as well as the opportunity to interact with leading scientists at the National Academy of Sciences.

The Savannah College of Art & Design (SCAD) is arguably the most comprehensive art and design college in the world. Each year, it hosts the SCAD Challenge for high school seniors and juniors "looking to get a head start in exhibiting their work on an international stage, as well as to launch their professional reputations as artists, designers or writers."[6] Winners receive a scholarship to attend the College. Winning scholarships range from $1,000 to $3,000 and can be renewed each year until degree completion. Another opportunity to compete for scholarship dollars in a creative field is the Art Institutes Passion for Fashion Competition. The competition is for students who have interests in fashion design, fashion marketing and management, and/or fashion retail management. Applicants' entries include original garments, design process book, the marketing and management of a retail plan, and a store concept. Winners receive up to half-tuition scholarships at an Art Institutes school within the United States or Canada. In addition, they receive a VIP trip to New York with a meet-and-greet at *Seventeen* magazine offices, $500 shopping-spree money at DKNY, and an additional $500 gift card.

If you are eligible to participate in any academic challenge or competition, do it! You not only have a shot at winning some money for school, but you also get exposure that may open up many doors for you: internships, jobs, invitations to conferences and meetings with respected people within that particular industry, and much more.

J) ***Recognize that YOU are <u>Unique</u>.*** We are all different and have distinctive characteristics that identify us individually. We were each made in God's image; thus, we were created in greatness and uniqueness. There's something about YOU that the next person doesn't have, and vice versa. Therefore, search for scholarships that cater towards those unique traits that you possess. For example, I have suffered with a skin condition called eczema all of my life. The condition, described as "an itch that rashes", is typically evidenced by rough, dry, and sometimes reddish patches on a person's skin. One particular scholarship that I came across was through the Inflammatory Skin Disease Institute (ISDI), an organization that promotes awareness of inflammatory skin diseases through education, research and patient advocacy. The Institute offers a $500 scholarship to a student suffering from any of the skin conditions that are included in the broad category of inflammatory skin diseases such as eczema, acne, and psoriasis. As an applicant, all you are required to do is to fill out the application and include the following: a letter from your physician or dermatologist stating your condition and its degree; a statement from your guidance counselor; and a one-page essay on how your life has been affected by your skin condition. Winning $500 couldn't be any easier!

Take full advantage of those unique qualities you possess that you would otherwise be discouraged by, as in my case my eczema. Do you have asthma, for example? Merck Respiratory sponsors the "Will to Win Scholarship" for high school seniors who have asthma. Or even more common among African Americans is sickle cell anemia. There are numerous organizations that grant scholarships to students with this condition, including the Kermit B. Nash Academic Scholarship and the Ohio Sickle Cell and Health Association. Juvenile Diabetes, formally known as Type 1 diabetes, is quite common in young people. Numerous organizations like the Juvenile Diabetes Research Foundation and the Diabetes Scholars Foundation award scholarships to applicable students.

Of course, there are many more unique qualities about yourself aside from ailments that you can capitalize on. Are you a twin or were you born from a multiple birth? You and your sibling(s) may qualify for scholarships from colleges like Sterling College in Kansas. Its Twin Scholarship Program allows for each twin or multiple-birth student to receive a 50% tuition scholarship as full-time students. Are you left-handed? Juniata College in Pennsylvania sponsors the Frederick and Mary F. Beckley Scholarship for left-handed students attending the school. What about your height? The Tall Clubs International (TCI) gives $1,000 each year to a student of "tall" stature. For women that means 5'10" or taller; men must be at least 6'2". Likewise, being short can get you a scholarship. The Little People of America (LPA) Association is a nonprofit organization that provides medical, financial and other forms of support to people of "short" stature. Members must be 4'10" or shorter. You qualify for an LPA scholarship if you meet this height requirement and if you fall into one of the three following categories (listed in order of preference by the LPA): you are a member of LPA with a medically diagnosed form of dwarfism; you have immediate family members who are dwarfs and are paid members of LPA; or you have dwarfism but are not a member of LPA.

My father served in the United States Air Force for 22 years, making me an official "military brat". Being a military dependent is unique enough to secure scholarship funding. I received the General Henry H. Arnold grant sponsored by the Air Force Aid Society for two years during my college tenure. Whatever makes you unique, whatever sets you apart from the next student, take full advantage of it! There is a scholarship out there for EVERYONE. Don't count yourself out. Do you research and be diligent.

*K) College Options.* A word of advice: APPLY TO AT LEAST THREE UNIVERSITIES. You may have your mind set on one particular college, but do not limit yourself by applying only to that school. Better financial aid opportunities may be awaiting you at other schools.

Consider the colleges your parents attended or are currently employed at. You may be offered a discounted rate for these reasons. Hampton University, University of Pennsylvania, and Princeton University are a few examples. Take a look at Duke University's Children's Tuition Grant Program. The grant is for undergraduate students who are children of employees, and it covers up to 75% of the weighted average cost of tuition. Children can use the grant every semester for up to eight semesters. If your parent has been working at Duke since 1975, whether as faculty or senior administrative staff, the grant will cover up to 100% of your tuition. The RIC Alumni Children Academic Award is granted to children and grandchildren of Rhode Island College graduates. Recipients receive an award of $4,000. There are many more scholarships for children of faculty and alumni out there. All you have to do is ask and research.

Once you have applied and been accepted to at least three universities, assess the financial aid package of each one. Each university will offer you different amounts of scholarships. Again, although you may have your mind set on attending a particular school, do not be naïve by overlooking this important factor. Remember, this is free money. So if one college is offering you a scholarship to attend and another isn't, be sure to include this in your selection process.

As Senior Class President who was an active member of numerous school and community organizations and held a GPA of 3.8, I was certain I would receive hefty scholarships from each of the four universities I applied to. However, this was not the case. The first school did not offer me any scholarship money. The second offered me $300, which was not even 1% of its $31,000 annual cost of attendance! The third offered me about $1,500 in scholarships. Hampton University, on the other hand, provided me with $6,000 a year with its "Merit Achievement" scholarship. The great thing about Hampton's financial aid package was that I knew how much I would receive even before the school informed me thanks to the listing on the school website of the various scholarships that all qualifying freshmen receive based on SAT scores and GPA.

Now this is not to say that Hampton is where you should attend college, but it is an illustration of the major differences in scholarship dollars that will be awarded to you. The $6,000 represented only about a quarter of the total annual cost of attendance, yet it was considerably more than the other three options. The most important thing I learned from this was that in applying to four schools, I was able to make a better decision financially. Had I been set on attending one of those schools other than Hampton, I would've limited myself in the amount of scholarships that I could've received. I would've paid much more each school year. Therefore, I was able to save a lot of money by applying to more than just one school and I was able to evaluate each financial aid package more clearly.

Also something to consider when selecting a college is the state funding that you are eligible for. Most states have programs that allot scholarships and grants to students who have resided there for a period of time and now attend or will be attending school in-state. My family and I moved to Virginia just before my 10th grade year. Because of my Virginia residency and my decision to attend Hampton University, a school within the state of Virginia, I qualified for the Virginia Tuition Assistance Grant (VTAG). This grant is part of a program that comes directly from the state of Virginia's budget. It provided me with money each semester to help pay for my education. The Massachusetts Department of Higher Education has a similar program. Its "MASSGrant Program" provides financial assistance to residents of the state. It even provides money to students of "nonprofit institutions" in New Hampshire, Maine, Connecticut, Vermont, Rhode Island, Pennsylvania, and the District of Columbia that have agreements with Massachusetts. The state of Georgia's HOPE Scholarship is another. It covers the full cost of tuition and mandatory fees for residents. It also includes a stipend for books.

Once you enter college, it will be easier for you to win national scholarships. National scholarships that are sent directly to your college indicate that those hosting organizations are specifically targeting students at your school. So unlike applying for a scholarship in which students from all across the nation are applying, such as those of Fastweb.com, these opportunities offer a greater chance of winning because the applicant pool is much smaller.

You have an even greater chance of being awarded a scholarship within the department of your college major. Not only is scholarship information sent directly to your university, but many hosting organizations also provide these scholarships to students of those specific majors within the university. Check with your department secretary to find out if there are any available scholarships from outside organizations for students of your major. For example, I won PepsiCo's Quaker, Tropicana, & Gatorade scholarship, of which the primary eligibility requirement was for applicants to be Business, Finance or Economics majors.

Lastly, recognize the partnerships that your potential colleges have with various scholarship organizations. This will surely have an influence on how much additional scholarship money you will have access to. An example is the UNCF (mentioned earlier) and its member colleges. The UNCF is the largest minority education organization in the U.S., providing scholarships, internships and fellowships for students at roughly 900 institutions. More specifically, it has direct partnerships with 39 HBCUs. This means that it is most focused on providing greater financial and career support for the students of those 39 schools. I cannot stress how influential this organization is in securing scholarship dollars for minority students, particularly African American students. Although such partnerships should not be a major deciding factor as to whether or not you attend a particular school, recognize that they do exist and keep in mind the types and amounts of free money that are available to associated students.

L) **City Governments, School Systems & Community Foundations.** The city you live in may sponsor scholarships to local students through governments, councils, and committees. A great example is the Peter F. Vallone Scholarship. It was established by the New York City Council and is awarded to New York City high school graduates. Students are automatically considered for the award when they apply for admission to the City University of New York (CUNY) and complete a FAFSA every year. Another example is the Newport News Democratic City Committee Scholarship. Applicants must be graduating seniors from a local Newport News, VA school. The recipient of this scholarship is also recognized at an awards ceremony and is featured in a news release that is sent to all local media outlets. Even school systems are now promoting scholarships for local graduates. As a graduate of a public high school in Suffolk, VA, I applied for and received a scholarship from the Suffolk Education Foundation. This nonprofit entity of Suffolk Public Schools provides nearly $13,000 in scholarship awards to graduating seniors annually.

Community foundations are also a great resource as they are typically established for the sole purpose of providing college scholarships. They acquire funds from donors, including local businesses and citizens. I received a scholarship from the Hampton Roads Community Foundation, which is an organization that invests and manages the charitable gifts that citizens of the community provide and, in turn, awards grants and scholarships with that money. A major benefit of receiving a scholarship from this community foundation was that it was awarded annually. The San Diego Foundation is another one. Through its Community Scholarship Program, it awards scholarships to graduating high school seniors, current college students, and adult re-entry students. In 2011 alone, the Foundation awarded $2.72 million in scholarships to more than 600 recipients.[7] Some foundations specifically geared towards college planning and resources waive college application fees for students with certain financial circumstances. Be sure to research such foundations in your area.

**M)** *Federal Government.* Agencies within and associated with the federal government provide millions of dollars each year through scholarships, fellowships, and grants. Students.gov is a great resource for this. Click on the "Pay for your education" link on the left side of the screen and you will find a comprehensive list of non-debt assistance being offered through these agencies. One particular scholarship listed on this site is the Department of Health & Human Services Scholarship Program. It is offered to students already pursuing graduate degrees in Primary Care. The scholarship pays for tuition, fees, and other educational expenses. It also includes a monthly stipend. In return, scholarship recipients commit to serving two to four years in an underserved community with the National Health Services Corps upon graduation and licensure of a medical degree. Fedmoney.org is another useful website in locating scholarships offered by government agencies. It lists, for example, the National Institutes of Health's (NIH) Undergraduate Scholarship

Program. Applicants must intend to pursue careers in the biomedical, behavioral, and social science/health career fields. Students of the program receive up to $20,000 in scholarship support, which can be renewed for four years. Recipients also obtain paid, summer laboratory experience and are extended employment at the NIH upon graduation, of which they must commit at least one year.

**N)** *Career Aspirations and Professional Associations.* There is a plethora of career-related associations that offer scholarships to students who intend to work in those respective fields. Whether your intended occupation is that of a doctor, a commercial pilot, or a marine biologist, there is an association for it. Research those organizations and find out if they offer scholarships. Chances are they do, and chances are you can win from your local chapter as well as from the national chapter.

I am a huge sports fan, particularly of college sports. I have such a strong passion for education, as well as helping college athletes realize their full potential on and off the field. A dream of mine is to become the first African-American female Athletic Director of an NCAA Division 1 Football Bowl Subdivision sports program (that's a mouthful, huh?!) During my last year at Hampton, I learned about the NCAA's Ethnic Minority & Women's Enhancement Scholarship. This scholarship provides funding for women and minority students who are pursuing a graduate degree that will propel them into a career within intercollegiate athletics, such as an athletic administrator, coach, or athletic trainer. Because I was already in full pursuit of attaining my Master of Business Administration degree, I could not apply. However, I would certainly encourage other women and minority students with the same passion to look into this scholarship.

Are you interested in becoming an accountant? The American Institute of Certified Public Accountants (AICPA) provides over 50 scholarships yearly to students looking to get their CPA licensure. Even if your undergraduate degree is not business-related and you would like to pursue a graduate accounting degree, the AICPA has a scholarship for you! A noteworthy one is the AICPA Scholarship for Minority Accounting Students, which provides up to $3,000. What about nursing? The National Black Nurses Association (NBNA) offers over 10 yearly scholarships ranging from $500 to $2,000 to students intending to become nurses. Winners even have the opportunity to be awarded at the NBNA's Annual Institute and Conference.

Don't discount scholarships offered by the military either. If the military is a career path you have been thinking about for a while, jump right into it! Your academic achievements in high school could secure you entrance into one of the five federal service academies, which are the equivalent of traditional four-year universities for public and private students. They are the U.S. Naval Academy, the U.S. Military Academy at West Point, the U.S. Air Force Academy, the U.S. Merchant Marine Academy, and the U.S. Coast Guard Academy. All accepted applicants receive full scholarships and are set to graduate with a college degree and a commissioned officer position, which automatically places them higher on the career ladder within their respective branch of service than those who join the military right out of high school.

Another way to get into the military with a college degree in hand is to join the Reserved Officers' Training Corps (ROTC) program at the college of your choice instead of attending one of the military academies. This route allows you to pursue your bachelor's degree while training to become a military officer at any college in the U.S. that offers an ROTC program of the military branch you're interested in. Some colleges may only offer one or two of the five service programs, however. ROTC cadets typically receive scholarships that cover tuition, fees, and textbooks, as well as provide a monthly stipend. Your military training will include ROTC courses, instruction in military operations, special programs, and physical training. In return for an ROTC scholarship, cadets make a commitment to serve in that particular branch after graduation for a specified number of years. As you can see, serving our country is very much a viable means of achieving a college scholarship.

O) *Google, News, Local Newspapers, and Trade Magazines.* Google for scholarships! Use search engines like Google and Yahoo to find anything and everything that may link yourself to scholarships such as your intended major, hobbies, talents and skills, intended career, etc. Be up-to-date on televised news and newspapers, as they occasionally publicize local and national scholarships. Also, pick up a few trade magazines every now and then. Trade or professional magazines include information and news related to a specific industry. If you're interested in establishing a career within the computer technology industry, *Computerworld* may be a great magazine for you to check out. Maybe you're interested in fashion. *BODY* magazine should be on your to-read list. Do you plan to work in the music industry? Always pick up a copy of *Billboard*. Trade magazines not only provide scholarship information and indirect links to scholarship opportunities, but they also allow you as a reader to stay informed about the happenings of the industry, which will prove beneficial as you matriculate throughout your major courses, complete internships, and eventually work in the industry.

Aside from trade magazines, more general magazines also provide scholarship information. A great example is *Diversity Employers* magazine. Launched in 1970 as *The Black Collegian* magazine, *Diversity Employers* is a career and self-development magazine targeted to students of color seeking information on careers, job opportunities, graduate and professional schools, scholarships, internships and co-ops, study abroad programs, and more. It is distributed at over 800 campuses nationwide. Another great example is *Teachers of Color* magazine. This national diversity recruitment publication is published biannually and distributed to 450 universities. It serves as a resource for prospective teachers, providing much information about grants and scholarships for students considering a career in teaching.

**P)** ***My thoughts on Fastweb, FinAid, and the Like.*** These particular websites host an abundance of scholarships for all types of students nationwide. Many prominent, national organizations have their scholarships advertised here. However, I would argue that you don't need to depend on these websites to win scholarships. The scholarships listed on these sites attract thousands and thousands of applicants across the country, making it increasingly difficult for you to win one of them. I am not discrediting these websites, as they provide excellent scholarship opportunities for students; however, I believe you will get much more out of your time by seeking scholarships from more local resources starting with your guidance counselor. He/she will be able to direct you on which scholarship you have a good chance of winning before you start applying, even if they're national scholarships that are listed on Fastweb like the Gates Millennium Scholarship Program.

Of the $100,000+ in scholarships I received, none came from these types of websites that advertise scholarships on such a national platform. My chances of winning were always greater when I was applying for local scholarships or those that may have been national but were sent directly to my school. The competition was less as the eligible population was smaller.

## Principle #3: Don't Be Discouraged By The "Little" Scholarships.

I cannot stress this principle enough. I understand you may be discouraged from applying for a particular scholarship because it only awards $500. What help will this bring in comparison to the $20,000 you owe for the school year? I know this is what you're thinking. I've been there. But you cannot let that deter you. Every little bit helps. Attending a college that cost $26,000 a year, it was sometimes difficult for me to focus my time and effort into applying for a minimal scholarship. However, time and time again those minimal scholarships proved to be just as valuable as the ones I received that came in larger amounts. I applied for a scholarship from the VSYDF my senior year of high school, believing that it only awarded $1,000 (roughly 4% of my annual cost of attendance). Little did I know that the scholarship was actually awarded to me at $1,000 per semester for up to the next five years of college. That $2,000 a year added up to a total of $8,000 I had received from the Foundation by the time I graduated. Imagine if I had not applied just because I felt $1,000 wouldn't do much to suppress my college expenses. I would have had to take out $8,000 more in student loans to graduate.

> _What the Community Foundation Director Says_: "Don't get discouraged. If you don't apply, you're definitely not going to receive the scholarship. There is _always_ a scholarship for you. It is important to not let the opportunity go by the wayside because you don't think an organization will grant you a scholarship. It may come from a local organization, the college you plan to attend, or the company you plan to work for full-time upon graduation. Don't get frustrated in trying to find the money that is there for you."

Another great example of a seemingly minute scholarship I received was the Naomi N. Malette Scholarship Fund, an annual fund given to my high school in memory of a local family's daughter. The Malette couple had a daughter who had graduated from my high school a few years before me and studied at another HBCU. She was tragically killed in a car accident before graduating. Her parents decided to provide the scholarship to a student who shared many of her same characteristics: an African American female of the same high school who planned to attend an HBCU and who was a member of the marching band—all of which I was. The joy in receiving this scholarship was not the money, however. It was the lasting friendship that I have developed with this couple. The mother even published a book about her daughter's life and she sent me a special copy. It is impactful life experiences like this that, had I not applied for the scholarship, I would've never come across. ___Luke 16:10___ *tells us,* ***"Whoever is faithful in*** ["is faithful in" is "can be trusted with" in other versions] ***very little is also faithful in much, and whoever is unrighteous in*** ["unrighteous in" is "dishonest with" in other versions] ***very little is also unrighteous in much."*** Recognize that God has much in store for you; but He wants to see that you're humble enough to accept the little that He is giving you now. If you are, rest assured that He will entrust you with more.

## Principle #4: The Essay Weeds Out The Weak, So MAKE Time To Write It!

Most students don't apply for scholarships because they dread writing the essay. I know what you're thinking: "It's time consuming and if I don't win, I would've wasted all of that time and effort." I've thought this on more than one occasion, but imagine where I would be had I allowed this thinking to dictate my actions by not writing the essays for the scholarships I won. I would be over $100,000 in student loan debt right now.

You have to change your frame of thinking! Always remember, scholarship money is FREE money. All you have to do is write the essay and fill out the application. Hosting organizations recognize that the applicant pool can be easily minimized by requiring an essay from applicants. So recognize that simply writing the required essay puts you in the small number of students who actually did the same. If I was an organization providing college scholarships and the only requirement was to fill out an application, I may need a secretary just to handle the amount of applications I would receive. However, if I mandated applicants to write a 1,000-word essay on how the scholarship is applicable to their lives, you better believe at least half of those applicants won't apply. They won't put in the time and effort to think about what to write and to then write it. And now, from an organization's perspective, I have a much smaller and higher-caliber applicant pool to choose from.

As a student, you are taking classes and dedicating your time to extracurricular activities. On top of that, you have college applications to complete before approaching deadlines. You may even have a part-time job. Needless to say, your plate is full! I understand that. But that does not excuse you from searching and applying for scholarships. If you want the money, you have to put in the effort. Many times, you'll find that organizations only require applicants to submit essays that are about 500 words, which usually take no more than an hour or two to type. I don't know about you, but I'm certainly willing to invest an hour or two to try to win a scholarship. In fact, one particular scholarship I received that fits this description quite well was the Dr. Jerome E. Bartow Scholarship. Sponsored by the National Urban League, this annual scholarship recognizes the contributions of the late Jerry Bartow to his corporate work and within his community. It is provided to three students of participating HBCUs. As an applicant, I was required to write an essay on what makes a community leader. I knew about the scholarship for weeks, but I kept putting it off until the day before the application was due. On that day, in between classes, I went back to my dorm and typed the essay in 50 minutes. It was 2 ½ pages long. I put thought and creativity into it while ensuring that it was a concise and effective read. I printed it and mailed it off. A few weeks later, I was one of the three students who won the $5,000 scholarship! In addition, I received an all-expenses-paid trip to the Black Executive Exchange Program (BEEP) Annual Leadership Conference in Atlanta that year.

All it takes is for you to apply. When writing your essays, have a positive attitude and an expectation that God will provide and that you will win. And you will! It has worked for me over and over and over. The essay represents the work, and God's Word tells us that faith without works is dead.

> *"What good is it, my brothers, if someone says he has faith, but does not have works? Can such faith save him? If a brother and sister is without clothes and lacks daily food, and one of you says to them, 'Go in peace, keep warm, and eat well,' but you don't give them what the body needs, what good is it? In the same way faith, if it doesn't have works, is dead by itself ... Wasn't Abraham our father justified* ["justified" is "considered righteous" in other versions] *by works when he offered Isaac his son on the altar? You see that faith was active together with his works, and by works, faith was perfected*[1] *... You see that a man is justified by works and not by faith alone. For just as the body without the spirit is dead, so also faith without works is dead."*
> (<u>*James 2:14-25*</u>)

You can have faith that God will provide you with scholarships, but if you're not willing to do the work, which is writing the essays, then your faith is dead. God has to see that you're willing to do your part before He does His part.

Lastly, do not be discouraged by a scholarship that you don't win. It is unlikely that you will actually win every scholarship that you apply for. I did not win every scholarship I applied for, but I did not let that stop me. I did not think to myself, "I wasted all of that time writing an essay for this scholarship, and I didn't even win." Instead, I understood that it was only one essay and one scholarship in the grand scheme of things, and the same essay could be tweaked and recycled for another scholarship (I discuss this in the next section). You'll come to see that trials like this will only increase your faith and build your perseverance for future trials. We are shown this in <u>**James 1:4**</u>, which states, *"**But endurance must do its complete work, so that you may be mature and complete, lacking nothing.**"* As you go through one trial, you are able to use all the tools God has already provided you with to be victorious. Once that trial is complete, you recognize that it prepared you

---

[1] God told Abraham to kill his son Isaac, his promised seed, on an altar as a sacrifice. Out of obedience, Abraham proceeded to fulfill this command. Just as Abraham was about to kill Isaac, an angel of the LORD appeared to Abraham telling him to stop. A ram was provided for the sacrifice instead. Because Abraham had enough faith and trust in God that he was willing to sacrifice the child God promised he would father, God blessed him abundantly and Abraham indeed became the father of many nations (Genesis 22).

so that you lack nothing that could hinder you from being victorious in the next trial. It is a continual build-up of your maturity and completeness.

> _What the Guidance Counselor Says:_ "You have to make time for it [applying for scholarships]. View this obligation as another class, and schedule it as such: dedicate at least an hour or two, three to four days a week, to searching for scholarships, filling out applications, and writing the essays."

## Principle #5: Be The STAND-OUT Applicant & Write the STAND-OUT Essay.

In order to win the scholarship, you have to be viewed as that one applicant who stands out far above others; and even if you don't, you at least need to be in the playing field. To accomplish this, take a look at primary factors that are considered in selecting scholarship winners:

- Transcript
- SAT/ACT scores (for some scholarships)
- Extracurricular activities
- Community involvement
- Achievements, awards, and honors
- Essay
- Letters of recommendation

Acknowledge these factors; do not take them lightly. Do your best to stand out in each of them if you truly want to be in the running for scholarships. Once you meet basic eligibility requirements, which are usually evidenced by your grade point average and the extracurricular activities that you participate in, the biggest factor of whether or not you win the scholarship is the essay. You have to write the stand-out essay. You have to present a compelling reason why you are the applicant that should be chosen. You must make yourself appear extremely personable, relatable, and more than worthy to receive this scholarship opportunity. The hosting organization needs to be fully confident that its investment in you will be worthwhile. How well you present yourself in your writing is a major deciding factor as to whether or not you will be selected.

But again, you must be a stellar applicant in each of these factors as a whole. Just as writing the application essay is part of that "works" in ***James 2:17*** I mentioned earlier, so also is doing your part to excel in each of these areas. You cannot expect to win major scholarships if you're not putting in major effort make yourself stand out amongst your peers. ***Galatians 6:7,9*** tells us "**. . . For whatever a man sows he will also reap . . . So we must not get tired of doing good, for we will reap at the proper time if we don't give up.**" Sow big and maintain your faith!

Here is an elaboration of those key factors that are essential in making you competitive when preparing that stand-out scholarship essay:

***Transcript: Maintain a decent grade point average.*** This is especially important if you are applying for merit scholarships—those that are awarded based on your academics. Always strive to excel in the classroom. Your effort will be reflected in your transcript, which shows your GPA and the courses you've completed. You don't have to be "smart" to receive a scholarship. With a 2.0 GPA, you are certain to get into college and to receive some sort of scholarship/grant money from colleges to which you apply. You may even qualify for outside scholarships. However, you will drastically increase your eligibility for scholarships by having a better GPA. For many scholarships today, a 3.0 GPA is the baseline to qualify. Thus, aim much higher! To truly make yourself stand out, strive for a GPA of 3.5 and above.

An easy way to increase your GPA is to take Honors, Advanced Placement (AP), International Baccalaureate (IB), or Dual Credit (DC) courses. I elaborate on these types of classes later on in Principle #6, but for now I'd like to share with you that honors classes are weighted more than regular classes, while AP, IB, and DC classes are weighted even more than Honors. This means that your achievement in these higher-level classes will have a greater positive effect on your GPA more than your achievement in regular classes, even if you don't do as well as you had hope for. For example, a C in an AP course will give you a higher GPA than if you were to receive a C in a regular class. You don't have to fill up your schedule with these courses; simply taking 1 or 2 and excelling in those courses will definitely drive your GPA up and help you during the college admissions process. What is also beneficial about taking on these exigent classes is that it shows admissions counselors and scholarship organizations that you are more serious about your academics than students who do not take them. It shows that you are the type of student who yearns to take a challenging curriculum.

Everyone is not an AP-type student, however. Many students are much more successful in regular classes. There is absolutely nothing wrong with this. It is your job to recognize the pace and level of rigor that you can handle when selecting classes. If you know you can maintain a 4.0 by taking mostly regular classes, and that your GPA may drop down to a 3.0 if you fill your schedule with these college-level classes (let's say you make all As in regular classes but all Cs in Dual Credit class, for example), I'd advise you to stick with a majority of regular classes. Having a great GPA is most important for scholarships and college admissions. No matter what level of classes you are taking, make the most out of your work and soar to your potential. The main goal is to stand out academically, whether that comes by you taking all IB classes, or majority regular classes with two IB classes, or half IB and half regular. With success in your academics, you will receive honors and awards that you can list on your resume. *Who's Who Among American High School Students*, the *National Honor Roll*, the *National Spanish Honors Society*—all of these are examples of recognitions that will come your way. Such recognitions will allow you to add more value to your scholarship application.

> _What the Guidance Counselor Says_: "Make sure you continue to show academic progress. Do not take Honors and AP classes your freshman and sophomore years, and then cruise through junior and senior years. And especially don't slack off during your senior year. Instead of only taking four classes or a study hall, maintain a rigorous schedule. Challenge yourself!"

**Work to get the best SAT/ACT score you can.** As is the case with your grade point average, you don't have to be "smart" in order to seize scholarships that judge your test scores. The better your test scores, however, the bigger scholarship pool you will have access to. Both the Scholastic Aptitude Test (SAT) and the American College Test (ACT) are standardized tests that assess the educational skills that students need to be successful in college. The SAT tests three components of a student's learning: critical reading, mathematics and writing. Each is worth a total of 800 points; thus, the maximum SAT score is 2400. The ACT tests the student's skills in English, mathematics, reading and science. The score range is 1 to 36, with the composite score being the average of these four components.

Either your SAT score or your ACT score will be a requirement for admission into college. For some students, it is natural to score a 2100 on the SAT or a 32 on the ACT. But for most, attaining a good score requires much effort on the student's behalf. Before you take either of these tests, take the Preliminary SAT (PSAT) or a similar assessment to see which test areas your skills are lacking. This will be your baseline for how to go about studying for a good score. Tools that can help you include: enrolling in an SAT/ACT-prep course, which may be offered at your high school or you may consider paying for through an organization like Kaplan; utilizing an SAT/ACT Study Guide, whether actually purchasing it or studying from it while enjoying a coffee at Barnes & Noble; signing up for both the SAT and ACT "Question of the Day", which is an email question that you can subscribe to have sent to you daily, for free, through those websites; increasing the amount of reading you do from newspapers and higher-level books; learning and applying new words into your daily vocabulary; obtaining frequent feedback on your writing from your English teachers; and working with your math teacher, perhaps during an after-school tutoring session, to polish your math skills.

I knew someone who scored an 1860 the first time he took the SAT. This is a terrific score, one in which he was comfortable enough to not try the SAT for a second attempt. However, I would advise you to take the SAT at least two times, especially if you know which areas you need to improve upon and you have a study plan. Most likely, your score will be higher the second time around and you'll increase your chances of winning even more scholarship money.

*Get involved!* Part of becoming that "well-rounded" student that colleges and scholarship organizations look for is to not only have a strong academic background, which is evidenced by your grade point average, the classes you take, and your SAT/ACT scores. It is also to participate in extracurricular activities. Such activities include clubs and sports at school as well as those you participate in outside of school like church and community work.

> *What the Community Foundation Director Says: "Belong to at least three activities every year. Show leadership by serving as an officer at least once a year. This doesn't have to be within a group at school; you may serve in a leadership capacity on a local committee, for example."*

It is important to not only involve yourself in extracurricular activities, but to also show that you have a passion for them. You do this by taking on a leadership role, dedicating more than one year to an activity, or even creating the activity! During my junior year of high school, I desperately sought a school club that had a strong presence in the community. After getting nowhere in my search (including joining volunteer clubs that were practically inactive), I decided to create my own. Founded by myself and two of my friends, the Volunteer Organization of Integrated Communities Envisioned (VOICE) became effective in February of 2006. I led as President and my two friends became Vice Presidents. We were heavily involved in our community through activities like cleaning homeless shelters, fundraising to benefit other nonprofit organizations, and assisting with the Special Olympics. The organization was so successful that it won "Best Club" at my high school a year after I graduated. The fact that I had created a club to satisfy my desire to be heavily rooted in the community provided an excellent talking point for my scholarship and college admissions essays. It helped my essays stand out by showing others that I was a passionate, creative, and ambitious leader.

Whatever you have a passion for, show it by getting involved! If you want to pursue nursing, assist your school's nurse or athletic trainer. If you want to become a politician or the next President of the United States, help coordinate local, state, and national campaigns. If you're interested in becoming a band teacher, take on a few solos in your orchestra and establish a more dynamic relationship with your band director. Colleges and scholarship organizations want to see that you are not simply involved, but that you are truly passionate about the activities you participate in. Show a connection between your activities and your career plans.

Keep in mind that it's not about the number of activities you are involved in as much as how active you are in those activities. For example, a student who is involved in three extracurricular groups, one of which he or she has a leadership role in, will stand out above a student who is involved in seven extracurricular groups but has no leadership position nor consistent participation. As with your academic achievement, becoming actively involved will also open doors for you to receive awards and to be recognized for your contributions. For instance, you may receive your basketball team's "Most Valuable Player (MVP)" award. Or you might be recognized as having raised $20,000, for example, for your church's youth mission trip. Having a passion, getting involved, and staying active in whatever extracurricular and civic activities you participate in will most certainly bring you some sort of public recognition.

Working part-time is not considered an extracurricular activity. It can, however, be used as a unique talking point for your essays. Many scholarships, especially those that are need-based, ask the applicants why they feel they need or deserve the scholarship. Your particular situation may be that you work after school to help pay the household bills. Hence, it is important to convey why you are not involved in extracurricular activities. Even noting on your resume your part-time job and the leadership responsibilities you have provides the hosting organization with a different glimpse as to who you really are. Again, your essay is about being personable. The organization wants to know who you are and whether or not its decision to support your education will be a good investment. This is simply another way to display that on your essay.

***Understand that how well you present yourself in your writing is a major deciding factor in being selected for a scholarship.*** Your essay is the resource that gives readers a view into your life and your aspirations. Therefore, be sure that you are presenting the best picture of yourself. Articulate your responses to the questions that are being posed in a clear and personable tone. What you write should not give a "bad vibe". You should not write about anything disrespectful or too personal. The content should be professional and appropriate to what is specifically being asked. If the application provides you with a half-page comment box to write your response, do not write one or two sentences. Fill the box; show the judges that you have much to say on the topic they are inquiring about, and that you are not trying to rush through the application. Read and re-read your essay to ensure that your words are organized and original.

If you are applying for a need-based scholarship, have a compelling case for support. Allow the judges to fully comprehend why you need the money. If you are experiencing real challenges in your household or within familial relationships, make them known. A compelling case only solidifies your need even more in the eyes of the judges. And articulating how you are overcoming your challenge also helps. The student who has a story to tell won't lose. I was a cheerleader during my sophomore year of high school. A fellow cheerleader, a senior at the time, was involved in a near-fatal car accident. With much prayer and support from the community, she was able to return to school some months later. When it came time for her to start college, scholarship organizations and donors couldn't wait to give her money because of the significant trauma she went through of being in a hospital for months and having to catch up on school once she returned. Even in the worst circumstances, God turns things around to work on your behalf, especially when you trust Him.

Once you have written your scholarship essay, have it proofread by an English teacher or someone with a good eye and excellent communication skills. You need it to be edited and critiqued. After writing a few good essays, you should be able to recycle them for numerous scholarships. Many organizations ask applicants the same type of questions: "What is your autobiography?" "What are your career aspirations?" "How does this scholarship apply to your life?" After having the template, you can replace choice words and rearrange some of the sentences to make your essay become the perfect fit for that particular scholarship.

*What The Community Foundation Director Says: "Don't have your mother write half of your essay or fill out half of your application for you because you simply did not make time to do it yourself. Organizations notice this. The language and writing style within the essay becomes vastly different, the handwriting throughout the application form appears not at all the same or is in different color inks, and so on. It shows that the applicant did not take the time to complete the application himself/herself."*

The overall package must be a winner. After you have written your essay, had it reviewed, and you're ready to mail it off, remember a few key things. First, be professional. A professional application is submitted on time and should not look like it was put together at the last minute due to procrastination. Stay aware of application deadlines and postmark deadlines, and the difference if applicable. In fact, the earlier you submit your application package, the more time the organization will have to contact you if your application is incomplete or if your package is missing a document. Most times, they want to help you to ensure that you have a good chance of receiving the money. So make it easier for them by staying ahead of deadlines. And if you don't understand something, ask! Ask your guidance counselor or call the scholarship organization directly. If for some reason you will not be able to submit your package on time, call the organization to let them know. This at least shows that you are open in communication and making every effort to win the scholarship. It gives you a greater chance of having your package reviewed instead of being overlooked due to it reaching the organization after the deadline has passed.

Be sure that all required documents (transcript, essay, letter of recommendation, etc.) are enclosed in a neat fashion. Any letter of recommendation you submit should be from someone who has a personal relationship with you. This will be evident in what he/she writes about you. Your first selection for a recommender should be a faculty member or an administrator at your school. Additional letters can be written by other people outside of your school, such as your youth pastor. By presenting your primary letter from a teacher or a school administrator, you show that you are serious about your academics. Obtaining a recommendation letter from someone of high regard should also be on your to-do list, so make it a point to establish a personal relationship with someone of this caliber. It will add value to your application. The relationship I had with my high school principal allowed for me to request a letter of recommendation from him, which he certainly accepted. Not many students have the luxury of having their principal write good things about them. Thus, his recommendation I sent to scholarship organizations and colleges provided me with another avenue for standing out above other students.

Do a last-minute check to make sure that you did not leave anything on the application blank and that you have followed all instructions. Following instructions is not an option; it is a requirement. It is part of the screening process. If the application tells you to submit two letters of recommendation but you decide to only submit one, you are placing yourself in the "ineligible" stack of applications. Also be sure your ink and paper are professional. Do not alternate between blue and black ink or submit your essay on pink paper. Some applications provide checklists. Utilize them! Lastly, put the correct amount of postage on your application package. Don't assume that it only needs one stamp. Be sure to get it weighed at the post office. Otherwise, it may be returned to your address and now you have missed the deadline.

***After the essay: Winning in the interview.*** Professionalism is to be carried over from your writing to the submission of your application package to the next stage (if applicable): the interview. Many organizations interview applicants in order to select the best candidate for their mission, goals, and investment. Often times it is the interview more so than the application that wins the scholarship for the candidate. My pastor shared that this was the case for him and a prominent scholarship he won while a student at Morehouse College. Just like interviewing for a job, come to the scholarship interview prepared. The night before, research the organization: its background, its mission and goals, the work it has done in the community and in providing scholarships, etc. Understand your role as a scholarship candidate. Be able to articulate your career goals, your interest in applying for the scholarship and why you are a valuable candidate.

Familiarize yourself with the traffic route so that you arrive roughly 15 minutes early. My Business Communications teacher in high school always told her students to "dress for success," and that's exactly what you want to do because it's always better to over-dress than to under-dress. As a student of Hampton University's Five-Year MBA Program, we were required to dress for success one to two times per week, depending on the executive guests visiting us. At times I thought the dress code was too strict, but the overwhelming comments of our guests representing America's top Fortune 500 companies were always of admiration and high regard. So I would advise the same dress standards in your scholarship interview.

For guys:

- Navy-blue, dark gray or black suit
- Light blue or white dress shirt
- Dress shoes and black socks
- Conservative tie

- Clean nails
- Presentable haircut and trimmed facial hair
- A watch as the only piece of jewelry
- Don't go overboard on the cologne

<u>For ladies:</u>

- A conservative dress or suit (navy-blue, dark gray or black)
- Light blue or white blouse
- Closed-toe dress shoes with pantyhose or knee-highs
- Clean, conservative nails
- No gaudy, flashy or long jewelry
- Don't go overboard on the perfume

Start the interview by giving the interviewer a smile and a firm handshake. During the interview, speak confidently. Provide thorough and thoughtful answers to the interviewer's questions. Remember, you've made it this far so the organization is definitely interested in giving you the scholarship. Remain cool, calm and collected. Maintain grace under pressure questions. Maintain eye contact. And most importantly, be yourself! Don't worry about the outcome; just interview your best and leave the rest to God.

## Principle #6: Be Smart With Your Money.

This guideline is all about making your money work for you when it comes to paying for college. Whether this is scholarship money, money your parents have saved for your college education, or money you're making at your part-time job to help finance your college education, the following are ways in which you can make those dollars stretch.

A) *Take college courses while in high school.* Take advantage of AP, IB and DC courses (mentioned in the previous section) offered through your high school. These college-level classes provide high school students with a great opportunity to get ahead academically before enrolling in college. The College Board administers 34 different AP courses. How many of those 34 you can enroll in depends on which are offered at your high school. Students of the IB Diploma Programme are required to take six exams of Higher Level (HL) and Standard Level (SL) courses in addition to meeting other rigorous requirements. Both IB and AP courses are free, as you include them in your schedule like you would any other class. If you pass the end-of-the-year exams, then you receive college credit which allows you to skip the applicable course in college. There are some differences between AP and IB curriculums. One may prove more beneficial than the other for you, so find out which set of courses your high school offers and do your research if you're considering either one. Dual-credit classes are also college-level classes for high school students, but instead of taking them at your high school you actually take them at a local college. Because of this, you'll have to pay the tuition cost of the course. This cost will vary depending on which college you take the course at. As long as you pass the course, however, you will receive the college credit. I took four AP courses in high school, three of which I scored high enough on the final exams to use as transfer credit in college (U.S. Government & Politics, Environmental Science, and U.S. History). This allowed me to walk into Hampton University on my very first day with 13 credit hours on my college transcript: my U.S. Government & Politics score accounted for one, three-credit course; my Environmental Science score accounted for one, four-credit course; and my U.S. History score accounted for two, three-credit courses. I used these credits for both electives and required courses.

B) ***Graduate a year early.*** If you are able, finish your four-year degree program in three years. Or if you're in a five-year program, as I was, finish it in four years. I certainly wouldn't recommend this to every student; only you know the course load you can take on without sacrificing your GPA. Finishing school an entire year early will require you to take extra classes in some semesters (which will increase your cost of tuition for those particular semesters), dedicate more hours to studying, and possibly take extra examinations to test out of some lower-level undergraduate courses. But the main point is that it will be worth it financially. I explain this in more detail in the next few sections.

At a high level, let's take a look at the financials involved in attending a public, four-year, in-state university during the 2011-2012 school year. Tuition and fees averaged $8,244. Room and board averaged $8,887. The average for books and supplies was $1,168. Transportation averaged

$1,082. And the average for other expenses was $2,066. That's a total of $21,447 that the student is paying per year.[8] Imagine saving **twenty-one thousand four hundred and forty-seven dollars** by graduating one year ahead of schedule! That is $21,447 less that you have to search and apply for in scholarships. That is $21,447 less that you have to save from your summer job or part-time job during the school year. That is $21,447 less that you need to take out in student loans. It is a $21,447 burden that you and your family will not have to bear.

C) *Enroll in a joint-degree program.* Joint-degree programs allow you to earn two degrees in an accelerated manner. You may earn a bachelor's degree and a master's degree within a total of five years, as I did with Hampton University's Five-Year Master of Business Administration Program for example. Or you may earn two bachelor's degrees in five years or both a Law degree (JD) and an MBA in three years, and so on. Colleges and universities across the nation are now implementing these programs, and they seem to be working quite well at providing students with a solid education in those respective fields. While in high school, start looking at schools that offer such programs if that is the route you wish to take.

As a business student, the traditional route for me was to get my bachelor's degree in four years, work in my career field for two years, and then return to school to get my master's degree, which is typically another two years of schooling. But I knew as a senior in high school that I wanted to complete as much education as quickly as possible. This was another reason why I chose to attend Hampton University. The program would allow me to obtain both my undergraduate and graduate degrees while being required to work at prominent companies through summer internships to add work experience to my resume—all within five years. This plan alone saved me from having to sit in college classrooms for another year while paying another school year's cost of attendance (5 vs. 6 years). The downside is that I would not gain as much work experience doing summer internships as compared to working full-time in my career field for two years. This was a disadvantage I was willing to accept, though. Even better for me, not only did I complete this accelerated program, but I did it in four years! This saved me much financial and academic stress.

D) *"CLEP" out of courses.* It may cost you $800 to take a course, but it only costs $97 ($77 for the test plus an approximate $20 sitting fee) to take a College Level Examination Program (CLEP) subject exam to "test out" of a course. CLEP exams, sponsored through College Board, hosts tests for 33 different subjects ranging from English literature to foreign languages to biology to information systems and computer applications. You can take an exam at one of over 1,300 colleges and universities. Usually the Testing Services department at the colleges administers the exams. The exam is 90 minutes long. You can take it at any time during the school year. And you are provided with your test score as soon as you are finished. If you pass, you will receive college credit for the course that corresponds with that particular exam subject. It's as simple as that. These tests save you time and an average of $824 ($8,244 cost of tuition and fees for a public, in-state institution divided by the average number of 10 courses taken per year). You can choose to spend 3 ½ months sitting in a classroom to take a course that cost you $824, or you can take a 90-minute test for $97 to skip the class and receive the credit. Note that you receiving the credit means that no grade for the course will appear on your transcript. Thus, your GPA is neither boosted nor negatively weighted.

I took two CLEP examinations while in college and passed both: Macroeconomics and Spanish. I would inform the testing services administrator at my university of the particular CLEP test that I wanted to take. After I paid the $97 fee, the administrator would schedule a test date for me, which was any school day I wished. For both exams, I purposely scheduled my test date within a few weeks of me signing up so that I could not procrastinate with studying. I had taken Microeconomics a semester prior to scheduling to take the Macroeconomics CLEP, so I was lucky in that I was already familiar with many of the linking concepts that are shared in both subjects. I chose to take the Spanish CLEP because I had taken this language in high school. For both exams, I dedicated a total of 10 hours to studying: 2 hours per day for five consecutive days. My study time was as follows: I would go to Barnes

& Noble; grab a Princeton Review, Advanced Placement (AP) Study Guide or CLEP Study Guide for the particular subject; sit at a table with my notebook; and study by reading, reviewing and taking notes. Over the next five days I would also review concepts and key terms in between classes and before going to bed. A bit of anxiety loomed over me for both tests, but relief and a sense of accomplishment certainly set in once I saw my passing scores. For the Spanish CLEP in particular, my score was high enough so that I would receive credit for both Spanish 101 and Spanish 102. Because the curriculum for my major required both courses, I hit the jackpot!

"CLEP-ing" out of courses, using AP credits from high school, and taking extra classes each semester allowed me to graduate one year early and save a total of $21,396. The cost-benefit analysis was simple: $194 spent on two CLEP tests, free AP courses taken in high school, and about $4,410 spent on extra tuition for cramming classes into a semester or two ahead of schedule = $4,604, compared to the $26,000 annual cost of attendance ($26,000-$4,606= $21,396 savings).

E) **Become a Resident Assistant (RA) at your campus dormitory or residence hall.** Many colleges and universities provide some type of financial assistance to its RAs, whether through partially paying for the student's tuition, covering room and/or board expenses, or simply paying the student a stipend. Resident Assistants serve as peer mentors and campus resources. Duties include: developing floor and dorm events; addressing issues like roommate conflicts, disruptive behavior, and adjustment difficulties; and assisting with administrative tasks. Take Elon University for example. It covers half of room and board expenses, as well as provides RAs with monthly checks equivalent to the other half.[9] So if this sounds like an on-campus job you wouldn't mind, give it a shot and save some money!

F) **Schedule your courses smartly.** Not taking a particular course in the semester that your curriculum has it scheduled for could save you money as well. At many institutions, full-time status for graduate students applies when taking 9 or more credit hours. Anything below that, the student is considered part-time and, thus, pays less in tuition. A friend of mine was scheduled to take 9 credit hours in the fall: two courses at three credits a piece, a two-credit course, and a one-credit course. In the spring semester, he was supposed to take 6 credit hours: two, three-credit courses. Instead of following the curriculum and paying full-time tuition in the fall and part-time tuition in the spring, he decided to take the one-credit course in the spring. This resulted in him saving $5,000 simply due to the difference in cost between full-time and part-time status!

G) *Use your breaks from school to your advantage.* During the school year, it may be beneficial for you to maintain a part-time job (if you are able). It helps to have this extra money for campus events, but it's also good to have it to pay for unexpected fees and necessities that may arise. Christmas break runs anywhere from three to six weeks depending on your school. Use that time to work so that you'll have extra money on hand to sustain you throughout the remainder of the school year. In addition, your 10-16 weeks off from school during the summer provides a great opportunity for you to get a job and save for college expenses or to start paying off student loans. Let's say you get a job making $8/hr and you work 30 hours a week. This equates to $2,400-$3,840 before taxes over the duration of the summer. Depending on what school you attend, this could easily pay off one to two semesters of room and board. And remember, every day that a student loan is in your name, it is building interest! So if you have the opportunity to pay it off before college graduation, do so. Even better than getting a summer job, you can utilize your summer break by . . .

H) *Getting an internship.* An internship is a real-world job experience for college students. It allows the student to work in the environment or industry that he/she intends to pursue. If I'm studying communications and I want to become a news reporter, for example, I may apply for an internship with my local news station. Internships are offered year-round, but are primarily recruited for the summer. Internships are much more advantageous than typical summer jobs such as working at a fast food restaurant or babysitting. Internships:

- Provide students with real-world experiences of what it is to actually work in the industry they are pursuing.

- Pay a lot more than typical summer jobs. According to SimplyHired.com, the average wage for an intern as of August 18, 2011 was $18.27, which equates to $7,307.60-$11,692.16 before taxes in one summer based on 10-16 weeks of work![10]
- Allow you to get a "feel" for the company and vice versa, ensuring it is an amicable fit for both parties. The purpose is for the company to train you so it can extend a full-time job offer to you upon your college graduation.

Considering that you get the real-world experience of the industry, you get paid over three times more than a traditional summer job, and you have the ability to secure gainful employment once you graduate, you have NO reason not to pursue an internship.

In addition, some companies even provide scholarships if you are accepted into their internship program, or vice versa (you may receive an internship as one of their scholarship recipients). The Association for Women in Sports Media (AWSM) is a great example of this. Last year's top applicants in public relations, broadcast, writing and copy editing were each awarded an internship and a $1,000 scholarship. Additionally, each received a paid trip to the AWSM Convention; which included hotel stay, reimbursement for travel and free convention registration. All other students chosen for an AWSM internship received a $500 scholarship.

ALDI, Hallmark, CDM, and Marathon Oil are a few other companies that host programs that provide both scholarships and internships to college students. Dominion offers a $5,000 scholarship and paid summer internship. The Central Intelligence Agency's (CIA) Undergraduate Scholar Program is available to high school students and college freshmen and sophomores enrolled in a plethora of majors from Business to Information Technology & Security to Language. After meeting stringent criteria, scholars receive up to $18,000 a year for educational expenses, internships with the CIA, and must commit to working for the agency for a period equal to 1.5 times the length of the company's support to them. My advice is to do an internship every summer during your college tenure. You may choose to do this with one company or with numerous companies. Either way, you are gaining the work experience you need to build your resume and to make you a competitive candidate by the time you graduate.

I) ***Enroll in a community college.*** While filling out college applications during your senior year of high school, you may also want to consider attending a community college for two years and then transferring to a four-year university. Community colleges, also known as junior colleges, are two-year institutions for high school graduates that serve as either an alternative or prerequisite to traditional four-year universities. The primary objective of community colleges is to academically prepare students for an easy transfer into their intended majors at four-year universities. Community colleges provide a wide range of majors for receipt of an Associate's degree. Many also offer job-training programs similar to vocational schools.

In the past, junior colleges were often associated with low-quality education. With the rising costs of traditional universities today, however, junior colleges are rapidly becoming respectable and prominent resources for students to obtain the education they need either for their career path (careers that don't necessarily need education higher than an Associate's degree) or before entering a traditional university. Because the first one to two years of college requires students to take basic classes, community college courses offer just that for a much cheaper price compared to traditional four-year universities. During the 2011-2012 school year, the average cost of tuition and fees at a community college was $2,963.[11] Compare this with the average yearly cost at a four-year, in-state public college of $8,244. Four-year universities are even offering scholarships to transfer students coming from community colleges. For example, a student of Community College of Philadelphia with a 3.3-3.6 grade point average can receive a $1,000 merit scholarship to Temple University. A transfer student from the same college with a 3.65 or higher grade point average can receive a $2,000 scholarship.[12]

As in all things, do your research beforehand and be aware of the partnerships your local community colleges has with four-year universities. If attending a junior college is the route you plan to take before getting your bachelor's degree, make sure your credits can be transferred to your intended major program at the four-year university you would like to attend. Note that at the end of your college career, you will have a diploma from the four-year university. Even your transcript will be that of the four-year university, showing transfer credits from the community college. So don't let the former stigma of junior colleges deter you.

On top of saving thousands of dollars in tuition and fees, most students who attend junior college also live at home and work part-time. This allows them to forego the cost of room and board (another $8,887 per year) while contributing money to their student account, paying off student loans, and/or adding to their personal savings. Some students even begin working full-time in their respective career fields while attending community college part-time, particularly if their job pays for it. I have a friend who was employed as an electrician apprentice at the Norfolk Naval Shipyard. He learned his trade by working full-time while the company paid for him to take courses at night a local community college.

J) *If you come from a low-income family and you have good grades, use it to your advantage.* If you come from a low-income family, obtaining an debt-free college education may be much easier for you than for students who come from middle-class or wealthy families. Apply to colleges that offer you free tuition. Nearly every Ivy League school—Harvard, Yale, Brown, Princeton, and so on—offer attractive financial aid packages to low-income students that include: free tuition, fees paid for, free room and board, no interest-bearing loans, and work-study, among others. The primary reason for this is because these schools want diversity. They want students who have the excellent grades but normally would not be able to afford their $40,000-a-year tuition. Plus, they are well-endowed. They have a strong alumni base that gives back financially. They also receive financial resources in partnering with corporations, government agencies and the like for a variety of purposes. As a result of the large amounts of additional funding and financial gifts these schools receive, they can afford to offer free education to qualifying, low-income students.

A good example of a school that provides such a program is Sacred Heart University. It offers the Fairfield County Tuition-Free Plan for Low

Income Students. The plan provides 100% tuition coverage to graduating high school seniors who reside in Fairfield County, Connecticut, whose family income is at or below $50,000 and who have been admitted to Sacred Heart University as a first-year, full-time student. To apply, students need only to fill out the FAFSA and the university's CSS Profile by February 15. Consideration is given to students who commute to campus in lieu of living in the University's campus housing. In fact, Sacred Heart offers its Curtis Commuter Award to entering first-year, full-time undergraduates who are Connecticut residents and commute to SHU. There are many different financial aid options like these that universities offer. Take advantage of them! Don't immediately count yourself out because you believe your parents do not make enough money for you to attend an Ivy League university.

Also, if your family's low-income status qualifies you for the Pell Grant, be sure to look into the National Science and Mathematics Access to Retain Talent (SMART) Grant. It is available for college juniors and seniors (and fifth years if you're in a five-year program) with at least a 3.0 GPA and majoring in any of the following: physical, life, or computer sciences; mathematics; technology; engineering; a critical foreign language; or a non-major liberal arts program. It provides up to $4,000 for each school year.

K) ***Borrow or rent textbooks, or buy used textbooks.*** Textbooks tend to be very expensive. If you are not aware of this fact now, brace yourself. You've spent the last 12 years using the textbook that your school provided. College is different. Your professor will tell you what book you need, and it is up to you to buy it from the campus bookstore, borrow it from a peer or upperclassmen, rent it, buy it used, or any other method in order to have it for class. My first semester as a freshman, I spent $900 on textbooks for seven classes. I bought each one from the bookstore. I was completely shocked at the idea that I not only had to buy my own textbooks, but that it would also cost me nearly one thousand dollars! After speaking with some classmates, I quickly learned about cheaper options. The next semester I spent about $300 on textbooks for another seven classes by buying from online sites. I haven't depended on the campus bookstore ever since.

Many professors will use the same textbook for a few years, which saves students money by allowing them to buy from upperclassmen who have already taken the course. However, there are also those professors who will use new textbooks for their course every year, forcing students to resort to the more costly alternative of buying from the campus bookstore. Even if I wasn't able to borrow or purchase a textbook from an upperclassman, my first alternative would be online sites like Amazon.com or Half.com. I primarily purchased used books, but even the new books at these sites were always cheaper than the new books sold in the bookstore. I never rented books, but I have many friends who did so with sites like Chegg.com. You can rent books and either access them online or have them mailed to you, which would require you to mail the book back at the end of the semester. A great and FREE alternative is to check out your campus or local public library. I've checked out a textbook or a novel that I needed for class from both types of libraries on more than one occasion. For textbooks you have purchased, you can sell them to your campus bookstore, to other students, or online once you have completed the semester and you no longer need them.

## Principle #7: Be Open to College Majors That Will Set You Apart From The Rest.

Your intended career has an influence on how much scholarship money you will have access to. I would like to stress the current need for students—particularly minority students—to pursue Science, Technology, Engineering and Mathematics (STEM) majors and career fields. Universities are freely giving out money to minority students interested in these subjects because there is a strong need for the next generation of science leaders and an even greater need for minority representation in these fields. For example, as of 2009, African Americans only represented about 5% of engineers and 6% of scientists in the United States.[13] STEM careers are a major component of the future of our economy. Being a person of color within these career fields provides job opportunities that are boundless.

Take my good friend and fellow "Hamptonian" Courtney. She chose to major in Chemical Engineering because she had a strong interest in science and math, particularly in chemistry. Not only is there low representation of

African Americans in this field, but there is fewer representation of African American females. This challenge was part of the reason why Courtney chose her major, and it paid off for her in more ways than one. She was able to attend Hampton University for free thanks to the university and major-related scholarships she received. She was selected to attend numerous conferences associated with STEM affairs. It was even at one of these conferences that legislators told her and other attendees that there will be a considerable amount of funding and scholarships invested into STEM and healthcare fields within the upcoming years. By selecting Chemical Engineering as her major, Courtney was also able to participate and lead scientific research on campus—beginning in her freshman year! Her research allowed her to work alongside her published professors, to present her work at conferences, and to receive awards for it. She did all of this before graduating from college.

The fact that Courtney attended Hampton University, a relatively small black college, made her scholarship and job search much easier than that of even other Hampton students. She graduated as one of only two Chemical Engineering graduates, both of whom are African American women! Because of this rarity, they both were highly sought after by companies and graduate schools who came to Hampton looking for Chemical Engineering students and only had two people to choose from. Additionally, Courtney was accepted into the esteemed National GEM Consortium where she received a fellowship (fellowships are scholarships for graduate and doctoral students to pursue their academic education and research) to pursue her Ph.D. in Engineering. Courtney leveraged the interest she had in math and science by choosing to major in a challenging, yet highly underrepresented subject. As you can see, it worked incredibly well for her.

I would like to highlight Shell, the energy and petrochemicals giant. As a student, you have a great opportunity to obtain financial assistance from Shell if you are majoring in any of the following sciences: geology, geophysics, physics, chemical, civil, electrical, mechanical, geological, petroleum, or geophysical engineering. If you are pursuing your bachelor's degree, Shell offers $5,000 annual scholarships to minority students through both its Shell Incentive Fund and Shell Technical Scholarship. If you become a recipient and meet necessary criteria, your scholarship becomes renewable for up to four years or until completion of your undergraduate degree. In fact, renewal of these scholarships is contingent upon you accepting an internship with Shell. So not only do you get the scholarship, but you also get an internship with the company. Even if you are a high school senior planning to enroll in an engineering or geosciences course of study, you can apply for Shell's Technical Scholarship Program. The scholarship is $2,500 and becomes a four-year renewable award of $5,000 upon completion of your first year of college.

Another highlighted company is Microsoft. It has been awarding roughly $500,000 in scholarships for several years to college students with a minimum 3.0 GPA pursuing careers in computer science or related technical fields. The company offers general scholarships, as well as scholarships specifically for women, minorities, and students with disabilities. Scholarships cover up to 100% of recipients' tuition for that particular school year. Recipients of Microsoft's computer science scholarships must also complete a paid summer internship at the company headquarters in Redmond, Washington. Academic majors and career fields in which minorities are not adequately represented provide excellent opportunities for students to receive scholarship money and secure a lucrative job upon graduation.

## Principle #8: Understand That God Knows Your Desires & He Knows What Is Best For You.

Just as a parent recognizes the needs and desires of his/her child, so too does God passionately care about what it is that you desire. He wants to give you more than what you're asking for. Even when you think you know exactly what you desire, you'll come to see that He, instead, knows what is best for you. The beauty in this is that what He sees as "best for you" is almost always so much more than what you could've imagined as best for yourself. Not only does He recognize this, but He makes it happen!

Hampton University was my #1 choice since the 9th grade for numerous reasons. My mom mentioned the university to me one day, knowing that we would be moving to Virginia (where it is located) within the next year. I kept it on my radar because I wanted to attend a college that was close to home. My mom also suggested Hampton so that I could receive the "black college experience" that an HBCU provides. I spent so many years living abroad in extremely diverse communities, which was absolutely amazing. Attending a traditional black college, however, would allow me to experience the "black identity" that I felt was missing in my life. Before finishing my senior year of high school, I made the decision to attend Hampton University. Now looking back, I see that God had so much more in store for me. I see that He wanted to add to my experience while supplying the desires of my heart that I didn't think to verbalize to Him.

For example, my dad got stationed at Langley Air Force Base the summer before I started 10th grade. Because of that, Hampton University became a 20-minute-drive from my house. In addition, my family and I moved to Virginia in proper timing, as I was able to receive the Virginia Tuition Assistance Grant by having been a resident of the state of Virginia for at least one year before enrolling into college. Also, the majority of the scholarships I received during my senior year of high school were only available to students living in that Hampton Roads area who planned to attend college within the state of Virginia. In addition, I gained a lot more out of the black college experience than I had anticipated. I attained a deep knowledge on the history and triumphs of black people throughout the time span of civilization. Self-knowledge and a true sense of identity were instilled in me in an effort to prepare me as a confident and competitive African American woman of the working world. Physical, mental, emotional, and spiritual tools from my professors and mentors were at my disposal to help develop me. Personal attention and enhanced learning was the structure of my education thanks to the small class sizes. Easy and frequent access to graduate schools and corporations that sought diversity was entrenched in the student experience. Lastly, I inherited a stronger drive for community service, particularly in providing for and mentoring the next generation of young black students and leaders.

In selecting Hampton, I knew what I wanted, but God supplied so much more: the ability to attend my top college choice which was in close proximity to home, and to receive more scholarship and grant money while gaining an enhanced HBCU experience. God causes all things to work together for the good of those who love Him (**Romans 8:28**). You can best show your love for God by the amount of faith and trust that you put in Him. I put so much of my faith and trust in Him to guide me in securing scholarships. Not only did He assist in that regard, but He provided everything I needed regarding my entire college decision and matriculation—more than what I could have expected or hoped for.

# 5

# IMPORTANT TIPS

## Be Aware of Scholarship Scams.

Greedy and dishonest people walk the earth. It's a fact of life. The world of scholarships is no different. Don't let this discourage you from applying for scholarships, but follow these tips to best discern which scholarships are authentic and which are not.

First and foremost, a scholarship should NEVER require you to "pay" for an application, a service, or any other type of fee. Do not use any scholarship or financial aid [search] service that charges you to provide information. This information can be accessed all across the web for free! If you or your parents are contacted by an unfamiliar organization that invites you to an "interview" or "seminar" about preparing and paying for college, do your homework. Ask your high school counselor or a college financial aid administrator whether they've heard of the organization and know if it's legitimate. In many cases, such invitations are a way to entice you and your parents to come and listen to a sales pitch: the company wants you to pay for advice on scholarships and other funding.

With identity theft on the rise these days, you have to be especially careful of scholarship scams that request too much personal info. If you receive a phone call on behalf of the scholarship claiming they need your bank account number to deposit your winnings or that they need your social security number to confirm your identity, hang up immediately and report the company.

Do your homework! Just because a company looks or sounds official, does not mean it is. Anyone can put together a document and insert the word 'Federal' or 'Association' on it to make it seem legitimate. However, if something doesn't seem quite right, be sure to search for the name of the organization online to make sure it is real. If you can't find any documentation of previous winners or previous award amounts, you may not want to apply. Most scholarship organizations want to promote who their previous winners are, not hide that information from the public.

· If you feel as though the scholarship application and accompanying materials were never proofread, move on. Multiple spelling and grammatical errors show a lack of professionalism that is essential to a scholarship foundation's success. Also, if the scholarship claims to be endorsed by the U.S. Department of Education or any other government group, do not apply. It is undoubtedly a scam because these groups do not endorse private businesses! Be sure to investigate any Better Business Bureau seals of approval as well.

If the company headquarters or the only address you can find for a scholarship is a P.O. Box address or a residential address, do not apply. If you can't even find a phone number for the scholarship organization, move along. If at any time during the application process you have a question that needs to be answered, ask the organization. If you receive a thorough and coherent answer, you're most likely dealing with a legitimate organization. If all you receive is the run around or if you are belittled in anyway, it may be time to move on.

If anyone, anywhere is eligible for the scholarship, it is most likely a fake. Scholarship organizations want to provide money for college students for a specified reason. The requirements do not need to be prestigious like academic or athletic ability, but there should be some requirements, such as being left-handed. All legitimate scholarships have some type of requirement. Also, there should be no "guarantees" that you will win the scholarship. Again, valid scholarships have eligibility requirements; any random student who applies should not have a guarantee to win.

If you receive scholarship information in the mail one day when you did not request it, it is most likely a scam. If you receive a phone call about scholarship information that you did not request, especially if the person on the line tells you that you've won, it is most likely a scam. You will usually only hear back from a scholarship organization if you have requested more information. Also, if there is serious pressure to submit your application by a rapidly approaching deadline, it may not be worth it to apply.[14] No one should make you feel pressured about applying (unless it's your guidance counselor or someone similar). Lastly, trust your instincts. If it sounds too good to be true, most times it is. If you naturally get an uneasy or unsure feeling about a scholarship offer, move on.

## Understanding the Free Application for Federal Student Aid (FAFSA)

The Free Application for Federal Student Aid (FAFSA) is the form the U.S. Department of Education requires you to fill out to determine how much financial aid you are eligible for. It is the government's way to assess how much financial support it will grant you for your college education. Primary factors that determine your financial need on the FAFSA include your parents' incomes, their assets, and the money they and/or you have saved for college. By reviewing these and other factors, the government is able to determine your Expected Family Contribution (EFC). The EFC is a figure that represents your family's financial strength. It is used as the basis for how much financial aid both the government (at the federal and state level) and colleges will provide you with. Types of financial aid provided based on the EFC include grants, loans, and work-study. The EFC is actually seen on the Student Aid Report (SAR), which is produced once you submit the FAFSA. This report also lists relevant financial information and is issued to you and the financial aid offices of your choice colleges. With this information in hand, the colleges can then create a customized financial aid package for you which you will receive as your Financial Aid Award letter.

The earliest you can fill out and submit your FAFSA is January 1 of every year beginning your senior year of high school and extending throughout your college tenure. Because federal financial aid is limited, it is granted on a first-come, first-serve basis. Therefore, submit your FAFSA as early as possible beginning January 1. As mentioned in Principle # 1: Start Early!, the government has a priority deadline of February 15 for FAFSA filings. All FAFSAs that are submitted by this date are privy to the federal funds and FAFSA information that the government releases on March 15 to colleges and universities across the nation. If you submit your FAFSA much later than February 15, you run the risk of receiving less money in your financial aid package because by that time, colleges have already issued a great portion of what they received from the government to students who met the priority deadline. Use the Federal Student Aid *(www.fafsa.ed.gov)* and Student Financial Aid Services *(www.fafsa.com)* websites as resources to help you better understand the FAFSA process.

If you are a student who is financially independent of your parents and you claim so for tax purposes, you are also able to claim independent status on the FAFSA. If you meet any of the Department of Education's criteria for claiming independence, then your parents' incomes and asset information is not considered in determining your financial aid. Typically, this will mean that you receive more federal and college aid. If for any reason your FAFSA is incomplete or inaccurate, which results in application rejections or delays, you are able to make all necessary corrections online or by phone. Visit *www.fafsa.ed.gov* as a first stop in doing so.

## Before-College Tips

1. ***Be a well-rounded student.*** Maintain a 3.0 grade point average at minimum. Take at least one Advanced Placement (AP), International Baccalaureate (IB), or Dual Credit (DC) course before you graduate. Aim high when taking the SAT, the ACT, and tests for classes. Every year, be an active member of at least one extracurricular activity (a sport or a school club) and one civic activity (church group or a community organization).

2. ***Apply for scholarships!***

3. ***Get your parents involved.*** Have them establish a relationship with your guidance counselor to receive college and scholarship information on your behalf. Encourage them to look out for scholarships for you. Involve them in your college selection process.

4. ***Go on college tours.*** Do your research beforehand. Find colleges that fit your personality, interests, and career goals. Have an idea of the colleges you are considering and visit them before the end of your junior year. Once you've narrowed down your choices to a select few that you are seriously interested in, visit

them by Christmas break of your senior year. Take your parents with you. Have an open mind and learn as much about the college, the campus, and the surrounding environment before making a selection.

5. ***Consider attending a minority-serving institution.*** These include: Historically Black Colleges and Universities (HBCUs); Tribal Colleges and Universities (TCUs); Hispanic Association of Colleges and Universities (HACUs); Asian Pacific Islander American Association of Colleges and Universities (APIACUs); and Asian American and Native American Pacific Islander-Serving Institutions (AANAPISIs). These institutions provide minority students with a quality education that is uniquely tailored for their respective culture, needs, and background. They serve as fertile training ground for tomorrow's minority leaders in all career fields. Although resources may be limited compared to Predominantly White Institutions (PWIs), the familial support and educational opportunities provided at these institutions offer an invaluable college experience. Many companies target them to fulfill their diversity initiatives, as these schools educate large numbers of quality, intelligent, African American, Asian American, Hispanic American, and Native American students.

6. ***Apply for Early Admission.*** Doing so takes some of the pressure off of you during the second half of your senior year. You will have the advantage of knowing how much financial aid you'll be given at each school, and you'll have more time to assess which college is the right fit for you.

7. ***Be strategic in your recommendations.*** Your recommendation letters hold leverage in the package you send to college admission offices and scholarship organizations. Your recommenders should be people of objectivity and prominence who have a solid relationship with you: faculty, administrators (for good behavior, hopefully), your pastor, and the like. To present yourself in the best light, leverage recommenders who will write about your best qualities, your achievements, and your potential. Be sure to give them ample time to complete the

recommendation, and don't forget to send them a thank you card!

8. ***Figure out your career.*** Many students have no idea what type of career they want to pursue at this point in life and that is absolutely fine. However, you want to walk into college being comfortable enough to have one or two career choices in mind. To figure this out, start by assessing your interests: What do you like to do? Assess your strengths: What are you good at? Take career assessment tests at your high school and local colleges. Check out the Bureau of Labor Statistics' Occupational Handbook at *www.bls.gov/oco/*. Meet people in the fields you believe you're interested in pursuing and ask them about their careers and their day-to-day responsibilities. Engage in job shadowing or volunteer in those career fields. The goal is to start your college career off right with an understanding of what career you plan to pursue. If high school graduation rolls around and you are still unsure, enroll in a major that you are at least comfortable with pursuing and that you know will provide a stable income and good opportunities if you continue to go that route. In the meantime, you are sure to stumble upon what you are truly passionate about. This will help you to not waste money.

## During-College Tips

1. ***Keep Your Parents Involved!*** I understand you're grown now and you don't want your parents all in your business. It is important to keep them in the mix of your financial situation and what you're doing within your major, however. Keep encouraging them to be on the lookout for internships and scholarships for you related to your major, your interests, and your intended career.

2. ***Remain well-rounded.*** You were a well-rounded student in high school because you wanted to look good for college admissions counselors. Now it is important that you remain well-rounded in order to look good for employers. Keep your grades up. Stay

active in at least one extracurricular activity and one civic activity. Acquire leadership positions. Be serious about your job search by enlisting the help of your campus Career Center, attending the Career Fairs, and following up with employers.

3. *Have the intent to graduate on time.* You are at college with one primary goal in mind: to graduate with your degree. Although college parties are enjoyable, they are not the reason why you're there. The longer it takes you to graduate, the more in thousands of dollars you will be wasting. Enjoy college life while staying on track to get your degree on time.

4. *CLEP out of classes, if possible, to save you time and money.* There is no reason why you should spend the hundreds to thousands of dollars on a course when you took its equivalent in high school and can simply test out of it. Total fees for the CLEP exam will cost you somewhere around $100, but will save you the tuition cost of the course and 6 to 15 weeks spent sitting in that course.

5. *Participate in an internship every summer.* Job competition is real, and it's fierce. You have a much better chance of securing the job you want with the company you want making the money you want by getting the necessary work experience before you graduate. Most students only complete an internship the summer before their senior year. Go a step further and look to obtain your first internship the summer after your freshman year. The opportunities are out there as more and more companies are providing internships for younger students. You will only make yourself more competitive in a tight job market by doing so.

6. *Don't stop applying for scholarships!* The resource pool is even greater for you now that you are in college as compared to when you were in high school. You have greater access to scholarships that are specific to your major, your university, and your intended career. I received a little over $20,000 in scholarships while in high school; I received over $80,000 as a college student.

7. ***If you haven't already done so, figure out your career.*** As mentioned in the "Before-College Tips" section, if you have no idea about what career path you want to pursue, then follow those same tips.

## Student Loans

I am not an advocate of student loans. I am a testament that more than enough funding from scholarships is out there for any student who wishes to receive it. However, I also understand that student loans do play a role in the college process. With all of the scholarships I received, I still had to take out about $16,000 in loans. Therefore, I would like to point out three things as it relates to students loans:

1. Accept <u>subsidized</u> loans. Unsubsidized loans should be your last resort. The federal government and loaning organizations subsidize the interest on subsidized loans, which means no interest will accrue on the loan while it is in use nor after you graduate. For unsubsidized loans, you (or your family) will be responsible for paying every penny of interest that is added to the principle of the loan. It is important to recognize the two and to use unsubsidized loans only when necessary. I accepted both types of loans. Once I began paying off my student loans, I found out that within 3 years I had accrued over $2,200 in interest alone for my unsubsidized loans!

2. Most loans provide students with a 6-month grace period, which means you have at least six months after graduation to start paying back any loans that you've accepted. So in the event that you are up in the air about what you want to do after graduation or are having a tough time attaining a job, you have the security in knowing that this financial burden will not kick in immediately.

3. Recognize that student loans are a part of the college process. Your goal is for you to get a college education. Although student loans should be your last resort, view them as an investment. Essentially, you are utilizing them as an investment to secure the job you want upon graduation. And that job should put you

in a place, financially, to be able to pay off that debt. In fact, many companies, and agencies of the government in particular, pay off all of your student loans in return for job commitment. The point is, don't let student loans deter you from receiving a college education, yet be responsible in the amount you take out so that you are not putting yourself in a tense financial position when it comes time to pay them off.

# 6

# THE CHARGE

The impossible is God's chance to work a miracle. You may feel overwhelmed in wondering how you're going to pay for a $100,000 education debt-free, but that's not your concern. It is God's. During my senior year of high school, my mother was very upset when she learned that despite all of my academic and extracurricular achievements, one particular college that I applied to was only offering me a partial tuition scholarship for my academics while a friend of mine with a C average and minimal extracurricular involvement was being offered a full-ride scholarship from the same institution on the stipulation to play in the band. I had a 3.8 grade point average. I was Senior Class President. I founded my own volunteer organization. I was on the basketball and cheerleading teams. I was thankful for the financial aid I would be receiving, but I was a pretty discouraged by it not being as much as I felt I deserved. Yet I remained completely hopeful that God would provide.

The scholarships didn't come in as I expected. I had anticipated receiving all of my funding up-front and having no financial worries for the next four years. But it took a period of four years to accumulate the $100,000+ that I received. I have come to realize that God may not provide when <u>YOU</u> want Him to, but He'll most certainly provide on time. **ALWAYS.** He wants to see that you will trust Him while you do your part (applying for scholarships). Looking back, I see that I did receive my "tuitions paid and full-ride scholarships" just as I had proclaimed at the start of this journey.

With three weeks left before my college graduation, I had a remaining balance of $3,289 on my student account. Commencement was scheduled for Sunday, May 8, 2011 and I had to be financially cleared by 4pm on Friday, May 6, in order to walk for graduation and receive my degree. It was Thursday afternoon, May 5, and I still owed $3,289. I waited for one of three things to happen within the next 31 hours: to hear the good news that I had won a $2,500 scholarship I applied for about two weeks prior; for a $3,286 student loan that I applied for two days earlier to be added to my student account (yes, it was $3 short of what I owed); or to receive the $2,500 scholarship discussed at the beginning of this book that had not yet been added to my account. As long as I got $2,500, I knew I'd be in the clear to settle the debt on my account. I prayed constantly throughout the day, asking God to provide me with the money I needed before graduation. I **PRAISED** and **THANKED** Him, in advance, for the blessing I could not yet see.

> *"Though the fig tree does not bud and there is no fruit on the vines, though the olive crop fails and the fields produce no food, though there are no sheep in the pen and no cattle in the stalls, yet I will rejoice in the LORD, I will rejoice in the God of my salvation!" (Habakkuk 3:17-18)*

With 28 hours until my deadline, $3,270 of my student loan came in and I now owed Hampton University $19! This isn't a testimony of support for student loans. As a matter of fact, the third option, the $2,500 scholarship, did come in. But it processed after graduation and, as a result, was mailed to my home. I knew that scholarship would come; I just didn't know if it would come in time to be added to my account before graduation so I made the decision to apply for the student loan. I still had faith that He would provide. He did just that. He showed me that He is still in control.

Our Father owns everything. All of the scholarship money you need for college is in His hands to give freely. Show God, by your faith and by your actions, that He can trust you with even the little that He gives you. *Luke 16:12 says, "And if you have not been faithful* ["faithful" is "trustworthy" in other versions] *with what belongs to someone else, who will give you what is your own?"* Once you show Him that He can entrust you with little or with what you acknowledge is not even yours, then see if He will not bless you abundantly. **Proverbs 28:20** tells us this in *"A faithful man will have many blessings . . ."* Will you do your part and apply for every scholarship that comes your way? Will you fully trust that God will provide exactly what you believe Him for? Will you stand firm on your belief, even in your most dire financial situations? This is the charge I give you. I tried Him, and He came through for me. I know He will come through for you as well.

> *"Don't keep striving for what you should eat and what you should drink, and don't be anxious. For the Gentile world eagerly seeks all these things, and your Father knows that you need them. But seek His kingdom, and these things will be provided for you." (Luke 12:29-31)*

# 7

# A SPECIAL GUIDE FOR PARENTS

***Parents: College is NOT an option.*** This was a common theme in my household. I am thankful to have parents who recognized that even in today's society, I, as an African American, would have to work twice as hard to be respected. College cannot be an option if we, as minorities, want to continue to compete in a global society and be considered just as intelligent as our counterparts. As a parent, it is your responsibility to steer your child in attaining an education.

This may be difficult for several reasons. For one, some parents may not have attended college and, thus, feel that because they are doing just fine, their kids don't need a college education to make it either. This is understandable, but today's economy is such that one must possess a bachelor's degree to even be considered for many jobs, let alone actually getting the job. There are plenty of people with master's degrees who are struggling to obtain a job because of the status of our economy. Most people today are obtaining master's degrees because they recognize the advantages of having a graduate degree within their respective career fields. More so than not, today's bachelor's degrees are viewed as high school diplomas, and master's degrees are viewed as bachelor's degrees. In order for students to adequately prepare themselves for a financially stable life and career, obtaining a college education should be a high priority. Doing so will open doors for scholarships, internships, jobs, and career advancement.

A college education is not for all, and it certainly is not necessary for all jobs. There will always be career fields that are self-dependent, whose services will not diminish regardless of the economy and whose workers will not need a traditional college education. Such occupations include mechanics, barbers, and entrepreneurs. In fact, air traffic controllers make over $100,000 a year without a college degree. However, some type of education and/or formal training is required for each of these professions. So as a back-up plan, and to provide your children with more opportunities in the future, encourage them to obtain some sort of college education whether it is a technical degree through vocational school or by attending an online college while they work in the professions they plan to pursue once they graduate. If your children are approaching high school graduation and are unsure of what career to pursue, encourage them to pursue something that is financially stable at the moment. This may be a solid job right out of high school where they can get training and educational support from their employer. Or it may include taking the traditional college route to pursue a major that matches well with their academic strengths and eventually filters into a stable career field. Preparing your children now, academically, will allow for a better transition into their career fields. Let's not forget that many people switch jobs and even entire industries throughout their working years. So for the undecided, preparing now by pursuing something stable will put them in a better position to explore different career opportunities later.

Another reason why it is difficult for some parents to push the importance of college onto their children is because they themselves are unfamiliar with how financial aid and the college system works. Parents feel overwhelmed by the entire process. This is very common. Hopefully I've provided enough information in this book to educate you on things like if you're approved for a grant, then you know you won't have to pay it back, or you recognize that establishing a relationship with your child's guidance counselor will help you with the process of attaining scholarships and understanding college financial aid packages. You should feel supported by the many scholarship resources and government websites like Studentaid.gov that I've mentioned in this book, as well as your access to the financial aid departments at the colleges your child is considering. All of these will give you confidence in understanding your role to help your child get into and be successful in college.

Working, raising a family, and the everyday occurrences of life do a great job in keeping parents extremely busy. After all of this, many parents have difficulty in finding the time to assist their children in preparing for college. This is a struggle particularly for single parents. However, when considering the dismal statistics and low expectations that minority students face today, parents simply cannot afford to be inactive in this crucial part of their child's life. Parents must continue to raise the bar. Higher education is the societal equalizer. The best way you can encourage your child to go to college is to be involved in his/her educational life as early as possible. Children who attend pre-school or a head-start program, who are physically healthy, and who have basic literacy, mathematics, and cognitive skills before entering first grade are more likely to attend and succeed in college.[15] If you would like to provide an exceptional education for your child but do not have the money to do so, be sure to check out options such as the Black Student Fund (BSF). Early Awareness programs are also helpful. Visit *www.finaid.org/otheraid/ earlyawareness.phtml* for some examples. By your child's junior year of high school, you should be taking them on college campus visits, making sure their grades are solid in time to start applying for scholarships, proofreading their essays, and making sure they are meeting deadlines. A parent who is this engaged will only help the student receive more scholarship money. If you're not proactive, the likelihood of your child also not being proactive is high. As the parent, you know your child best. So, in the words of my mom, "If your child has even an inkling of talent in him, then you need to be out there researching, getting information, building relationships and networking for scholarship opportunities, and finding ways that will allow your child to capitalize on his/her strengths, talents, and interests for scholarship dollars."

Making time for these key activities, as a parent, will greatly enhance your child's opportunities in transitioning into college (some of these are elaborated later on):

1.  Spend a few moments at home every day reviewing your child's academic progress and grades. Make sure they are striving for and maintaining at least a 3.0 grade point average.
2.  Establish a relationship with his/her guidance counselor.

3. Dedicate time on the weekends to review college and scholarship applications.
4. Make sure your child is actively involved in at least one extracurricular club and one civic/community-based club.
5. Have faith that God will provide for your child to attend college.

***Parents: Take a serious role in planning—financially—for your child's college education.*** In a perfect world, you would begin saving for your child's college expenses at the time of his/her birth. But realistically, this doesn't happen frequently. Oftentimes, life dictates otherwise. So whether your child was born two weeks ago or is about to graduate from high school, start saving! That money will come in handy once your child is in college. Even if you save and your child decides not to attend college, that money is still at your disposal. It's better to save and be in a position to help your child than to not save and find yourself consistently in a bind to support him/her. Gone are the days in which students can easily pay their way through college. As a parent, the money you contribute towards your child's college education will go a long way. It doesn't matter how much you can contribute, just as long as there is *something* to contribute. Even if you don't believe in paying for your child's college education, recognize that every little bit helps to put your child in a better financial position to attain a college degree. Save by making regular contributions. Remember that the goal is to help the next generation become more successful and more prosperous than your generation. Part of that goal is encouraging your child to attend college, and then supporting him/her with your finances. In doing so, you are helping him/her to avoid taking out student loans and getting into binds when faced with tough financial times at college.

Today, parents can utilize state-funded 529 college savings account plans to save for college expenses. These plans allow parents to contribute money, either automatically or on occasion, to an interest-bearing account that holds underlying mutual funds and similar investments. Other types of 529 plans allow you to "pre-pay" the cost of a college education by buying the tuition at today's prices. The interest rate is typically compounded which equals greater return than a traditional savings account. You can compare interest rates state-by-state and open up a 529 with the plan that you are most comfortable with, even if you do not live in that state. 529 plans are intended for college purposes only; thus, there is a 10% tax penalty if the money is used for anything else. Opening such an account for your child also allows others to get involved. Grandparents, other family members, and friends can all contribute. You can ask them to contribute when they are trying to think of birthday and Christmas gifts for your child, for example. There are also tax incentives to investing in a 529 plans, including that the money grows tax-free (on the federal level) and can be withdrawn tax-free.[16] These plans are good because they are considered a "parental asset" on the FAFSA, which only accounts for 5.64% in determining a student's EFC. The EFC is the primary basis for the government and colleges to assess how much money the student has available before receiving federal financial aid, so students with lower EFCs receive more financial aid. A parent who has saved $50,000 in a 529 college savings plan for his/her child, yet no other savings, can expect to still receive a solid financial aid package because of that low 5.64% factor.

529 plans are even better when they are opened by family members other than the parents. In this circumstance, the money has no effect on your child's eligibility for federal financial aid. Let's say you have only saved $2,000 in a savings account for your child's college expenses. This savings is an asset and you would document it as part of the EFC. The FAFSA, however, does not inquire about assets belonging to anyone other than you or your child, regardless of whether those other assets are for your child. Now let's say that your parents (your child's grandparents) open a 529 account for your child, and it has accrued $30,000. That $30,000 is not acknowledged as part of the EFC and, thus, shows the government that you only have $2,000 to contribute towards your child's college education. This then puts your child in a position to receive a great deal of financial assistance from the government, although in reality he/she will still have $30,000 at his/her disposal. However, distributions of that account may be treated as taxable income to the beneficiary (your child), so be sure to do your research. The good thing about 529 savings plans is that if your child decides not to attend college, the funds can be deposited into another child's 529 plan or to pay for educational expenses of the owner, whether that is you or your grandparents.

529 accounts are also attractive because some states actually match a portion of your contributions. Most of the matching contributions work such that the state matches anywhere from 33% to 100%, dollar for dollar, of the parents' investment. Minnesota, Louisiana, Utah, Colorado, Arkansas, Nevada, Rhode Island, Kansas, Maine and North Dakota all provide a financial match for residents who invest in state 529 plans. Although there is a limit to matches, most participating states will contribute somewhere around $500 to $600 maximum per year toward the college savings. Several matching programs only apply to low- or middle-income parents. Some state 529 programs even provide their own scholarships. Georgia's Path2College 529 College Savings Plan, for example, hosts its annual "Destination College Savings Sweepstakes." In partnership with the Georgia Public Library Service, the Sweepstakes awards a $5,529 financial contribution to a Path2College savings account. The 2011 winner was a seven-year-old!

Nowadays, 529 plans are becoming more innovative. An example is the Gerber Life College Plan. It works as both a college savings plan and adult life insurance. Owners contribute monthly payments to it as they would for traditional life insurance. The money incurs stable growth with a guaranteed value so that the payout can be up to $150,000. The innovative segment of this plan is that the money has the flexibility to be used for college expenses or for anything else without suffering a 10% tax penalty.[17]

529 savings plans serve as a common investment vehicle to build a nest egg for your child's college education. I am not advising you to open one, but certainly look into them and do adequate research to weigh the pros and cons if this sounds like something you would be interested in. For parents who are completely comfortable in financially providing for their child's college education, a 529 plan may be the way to go. However, many parents do not plan to or cannot adequately foot the bill of their child's education—and rightfully so. The intention is to encourage every child to attain a college degree, but obviously not all children will do so. Some of the brightest kids are more comfortable with heading right into the workforce after high school and maybe getting a degree a few years down the road. Perhaps some are more comfortable completing the necessary training to obtain certification for their particular career field. Considering these and similar circumstances, many parents do not want to put money into a 529

savings account. If their child does not attend college and the parents have contributed to such a plan, then they are now subject to a 10% tax penalty for withdrawing the money they invested for purposes other than paying for college. For the parent who wishes to remain cautious due to not knowing his/her child's career plans or has made the decision to not pay for his/her child's college education, recognize that it is still beneficial to establish some sort of savings plan. You may be more comfortable with making regular contributions to a savings account, a money market account, or a mutual fund to build money for future college expenses. Parents who start some sort of savings plan for their child's college education wind up with more savings, more interest, and less stress in being able to provide than parents who wait even a few years later.

One financial advantage for parents of college students is that they can claim additional credits for college expenses during tax season. The American Opportunity Tax Credit allows parents to qualify for a tax credit up to $2,500, $1,000 of which is refundable if the child is still considered a dependent for tax purposes. Students who are no longer considered dependents and who pay their own taxes also qualify for this credit. The main requirement is that the adjusted gross income (AGI) cannot exceed $80,000 a year for individuals filing taxes separately or $160,000 a year for couples filing jointly. The American Opportunity Tax Credit provides coverage up to the first four years of post-secondary education. It is an extension of the Hope Credit, which provides a $1,800 tax credit for up to the first two years of college. The third tax credit available to parents and students is the Lifetime Learning Credit, which provides a non-refundable, maximum of $2,000 per year for educational expenses. It is limited to individuals with AGIs of no more than $50,000 if filing single or $100,000 if filing jointly. Of course, you can only claim one of these credits per year. Research which credit, according to your tax liability, is most beneficial for you.

Another avenue to utilize the federal government help foot the bill of your child's college education is through grants, specifically the Federal Pell Grant and the Federal Supplemental Educational Opportunity Grant. The Federal Pell Grant uses the EFC to determine low-income status of the family and the financial need of the student. It offers a maximum of $5,500 per student per year. Students with the lowest EFCs, considered having "exceptional need", have priority for the Federal Supplemental Education Opportunity Grant, which provides additional grant money valued up to $4,000! The FAFSA will determine if your child is eligible for either grant. Your job is to fill out the FAFSA for him/her as early as possible after January 1.

*Parents: Encourage your child to get involved in the community.* It is important to develop a volunteer in your child, which helps to create a well-rounded resume. Organizations that provide scholarships want to see that their money is going towards a great investment: a sharp student whose grades are just as amazing as his/her volunteer work. Being involved in the community will only increase the chances of your child winning scholarships.

*Parents: Establish a relationship with your child's guidance counselor or scholarship coordinator around his/her junior year.* This is the first and foremost step in showing that you are fully engaged in helping your child secure as much external funding as possible for college. Such a relationship will allow you to create a rapport with the counselor that will prove beneficial during much-needed times. For example, your child may submit a scholarship application late and need that relationship with his/her counselor to push the application through to the organization. Or the counselor might have no students applying for a particular scholarship, and call you directly to encourage your child to apply.

*Parents: Make yourselves aware of scholarships just as students do.* Many school websites list scholarship information online or enable parents to receive email updates for them. Take advantage of this. Additionally, research scholarships online. Ask your employer, church, volunteer group or other associations if they either offer scholarships or if they know of any. Being a proactive parent serves as tremendous help for students who are busy with school, involved in extracurricular activities, or may be applying for numerous scholarships all at the same time. There is no way I would have won all of the scholarships I did without my mother constantly asking me questions like, "Did you apply for this scholarship?" and "You know the deadline for this scholarship is in three days, right?" She prayed for my scholarships, she researched scholarships for me to apply to, she reminded me of deadlines, and she even mailed the applications out when I could not. Having a parent like that was crucial throughout the entire process. Parents, do all you can to ensure your child wins all the scholarship money that he/she is entitled to!

# 8

# MEET THE PERSON I CREDIT MY SCHOLARSHIP SUCCESS TO

I hope this book was a blessing to you. I pray that you are able to take every tip, advice and thought I've presented and use it to build your faith in winning scholarships for college. But I cannot take the credit for what I've been blessed to share. There is only one person who made it possible for me to be where I am and to encourage others. His name is Jesus. He is a personal friend of mine—and so much more. He comforts me when I am hurt, concerned, worried, and discouraged. He reassures me of who I am, how much He loves me, and that He is always at my side in the midst of my trials. In fact, He <u>carries</u> me when I feel like I can't even take another step while in the storm. There is no way I could've maintained persistence in my scholarship endeavors without His continual assurance and guidance.

Jesus encourages me to keep pressing with faith because there will be a blessing at the end, which is why I can encourage you. ***1 Peter 5:10-11*** says ***"Now the God of all grace, who called you to His eternal glory in Christ Jesus, will personally restore, establish, strengthen, and support you after you have suffered a little. The dominion belongs to Him forever. Amen."*** Through Jesus, we can rest assured knowing that God's love and grace will cover us and bless us after having stood through the storm. Whether you're worrying about how you're going to pay for college or you're dealing with a different hardship that throws itself unexpectedly your way, know that it is just a test. Your faith will show God how much you love him back. ***James 1:12*** says, ***"A man who endures trials is blessed, because when he passes*** *the test he will receive the crown of life that God has promised to those who love Him."*

There is a bigger picture to this: we have access to Jesus. Because God loves us so dearly, He sent his Son to earth to suffer in our sufferings and to die on a cross so that we may receive that eternal crown of life in heaven one day. All you have to do is take advantage of that access by accepting Jesus into your heart and acknowledging Him as your Savior—the one whom God sent to save you from a life of sin, which is a life separated from Him. Find completeness by surrendering your life to Jesus. Allow Him to lead you through all of the good and bad that you will experience during your journey here on earth. Submit yourself to God's will and see that He will provide more than you could've ever asked for or imagined *(Ephesians 3:20)*. This world and the things of it are so fleeting and movable, so why not give in to the only immovable power? Why not trust in God, who said in *Jeremiah 1:5, "I chose you before I formed you in the womb; I set you apart before you were born . . ."* Why not trust in God who said in *Jeremiah 29:11, "For I know the plans I have for you . . . plans for your welfare, not for disaster, to give you a future and a hope. You will call to Me and come and pray to Me, and I will listen to you. You will seek Me and find Me when you search for Me with all your heart. I will be found by you . . . and I will restore your fortunes and gather you from all the nations and places where I banished you . . ."* He knows you best and He has a plan for you. I encourage you, today, to enter into a relationship with Jesus and to give God's will for your life a try. Doing so was the greatest decision I made and will ever make; and He has not failed me yet. It's as simple as saying this prayer:

*"Lord Jesus, I acknowledge that I am a sinner in need of a savior. I ask you to forgive me of all my sins, and to live in my heart. From this day forward I acknowledge you as my Lord and my Savior and by your grace, I will serve you for the rest of my life. In Jesus Name, I pray, Amen."*[18]

The Word tells us that anything we ask for in Jesus' name will be done *(John 13:13-14)*. By you genuinely praying the prayer above, you have accepted Jesus into your heart! I rejoice and celebrate with you in your salvation. But know that the LORD is rejoicing even more! I encourage you to connect with a church and to ask God to place people in your life who will help you grow and mature in Christ. Be blessed!

# 9

# TESTIMONIES: GOD PROVIDED FOR THESE STUDENTS TOO!

I am certainly not the only student who ever stood on his/her faith in believing that God would provide scholarship money for college. I am blessed to be able to share my personal experience, but I would also like to highlight how God provided for two of my classmates as well. I hope you are encouraged!

## Lorreanne Webley, Hampton University Class of 2010

I must've applied for every scholarship on Fastweb. I never received one. But I would like to share my experience with two scholarships I did receive from other resources—one during my freshman year and the other during my last year at Hampton University.

During my freshman year at Hampton, I only had enough money to cover my expenses for the first semester. My mother entered into a Susu (aka "partners") account on my behalf with some of her friends and associates. Partners is a common saving tradition amongst West Indian and African peoples. The way it worked for my mother was: a group of fifteen parents who also had children in college or were heading to college agreed to become members of the account; each month, everyone contributed an equal amount of $200; each month, all of the money ($3,000) went to one parent; the following month, all of the money went to the next parent, and so on. So from this, I used my $3,000 to pay towards tuition and fees for my first semester at Hampton.

I knew finances would be tight and I didn't want to be a burden on my parents, so I got a job at McDonalds early on in the first semester. By October, it was clear that I would have about $1,500 outstanding to pay for the second semester. It just seemed like there was no way I nor my parents would be able to meet this need. I am the fourth child of six, and two of my older siblings were also in school at this time. My parents were not only paying for their tuition but also co-signing on their student loans. So because of this, student loans weren't even an option for me; I couldn't get a co-signer for any, not even Sallie Mae loans! And to make things worse, I had submitted my FAFSA late that year, so I was not awarded any student loans in my financial aid package. In addition, my eldest sibling and his own family were going through a tough financial time, so my parents stepped in to support the four of them.

I applied to Binghamton University that October, and in November I applied for the Hampton University Long Island Chapter Alumni Scholarship, which was about $1,700. I figured I would either win this scholarship, which I had applied for on the deadline date, or I would go back home to attend school. I didn't want to get stuck in the circumstance of taking a semester off from school so attending Binghamton, an in-state institution and a school with many financial resources for minority students (both of which are applicable to me), would allow me to go to school practically for free. Although Hampton University was where my heart lay, Binghamton became my Plan B. My mother and I discussed our financial situation and the fact that there was no more Partners money to be used for the second semester. Our agreement was that if we could pay for it, then I would be able to stay at Hampton.

All I had my mind on was completing at least one year at Hampton, and then I would be able to confidently and comfortably transfer to Binghamton. In December, I was accepted. Although relieved, this was not what I truly wanted. I went home for Christmas break not knowing where I would be by the time spring semester came. This is when I started relying on my heavenly Father to make a way for me. I was praying so hard for the Alumni Scholarship every single night. "Jesus, let me get the scholarship. Please! Forgive me. Bye." I laugh at my concise and seemingly insensitive prayer as I look back on it now, but at the time this was my genuine prayer. I put all of my trust in God, believing that He would provide. I started becoming confident, saying to myself "I'm going to get the scholarship." I even had people at my church praying for me. And of course, my parents were praying like crazy.

All throughout Christmas break I did not hear back from the Chapter Alumni for the scholarship. I had to return to Hampton the week of January 8. Six days before classes resumed at Hampton, I found out that I would be the recipient of the scholarship! Talk about receiving a blessing right on time! That was exactly when I needed it the most. And when I received my scholarship, I actually got a refund—a portion back of the total scholarship! Scholarships are usually broken up so that the student receives half of it during the first semester and the other half during the second semester. Because my scholarship was applied to my student account just for the second semester, however, it paid off my outstanding balance and gave me the remaining amount as a refund. At that time, I could not see that this experience of having my faith tested would prepare me for the next test during my final year at Hampton.

As a student of the Five-Year MBA Program, my final year at Hampton was my graduate year. During my sophomore, junior and senior years, the Partners amount had increased to $6,000 per parent, which my mother provided for me during those years. But by my graduate year, I had two younger siblings in high school who would soon be heading to college and so I wanted that year's money to go to the next younger sibling. I was fortunate enough, however, to receive the Pell Grant as well as have access to student loans. Any remaining balance on my student account I told my mother I would pay for, whether it would be via additional loans, getting a job, or working a graduate assistantship. By this time, I was so much stronger in my faith than freshman year. I kept telling myself, "God worked it out then, and He will work it out now." I would repeatedly listen to Hezekiah Walker's song "God Favored Me" and "Smokie" Norful's "I Need You Now".

I went back to Hampton one month early in an attempt to obtain a graduate assistantship. I looked everywhere, in every department, but all I kept getting were "No's". My parents, feeling sorry for me, decided that they would help me pay for school. They were doubtful that I would get the money I needed, but my confidence said, "I'm going to get it." One day in September, I was provoked to check for graduate assistantships in the student center. I met with one of the student activities advisors and was offered the assistantship. Immediately, this allowed me to pay off 30% of my tuition. At the end of the first semester, however, I lost the graduate assistantship. My next option was to take out a Grad PLUS loan with 13% interest. Before I could even apply for it, though, I was awarded a scholarship from the School of Business. The $2,000 award is provided annually to all graduate students of the Five-Year MBA Program, without any of us being required to apply! I knew nothing about this scholarship before then, so I was absolutely overwhelmed when I heard the wonderful news. With that, the balance I had on my student account became fully paid for. I was so thankful!

I truly believe it was my faith, my prayers, and my confidence that allowed me to receive both scholarships. My faith was a bit shaky freshman year; by graduate year, my faith did not waiver one bit. I knew, although my circumstance looked slim, that God didn't do what He did my freshman year for no reason. I knew He would pull through for me. My faith was strengthened from freshman year to that time because of what He had done.

I would encourage students in similar circumstances to pray and to never stop believing that they are going to be blessed. Start speaking it. Start telling yourself, "I am going to get it." In this, you are convincing yourself so that when you start praying, your prayer is strengthened. It's like you telling God, "God, You're going to do this." Even **_Matthew 21:21-22_** speaks of this saying, _**"Jesus answered them, 'I assure you: If you have faith and do not doubt, you will not only do what was done to the fig tree, but even if you tell this mountain, 'Be lifted up and thrown into the sea,' it will be done. And if you believe, you will receive whatever you ask for in prayer.'"**_

You have to develop a "no other way" mentality that says, "I have to win this scholarship. There is no way I can be denied." Everything changes when your mentality changes to that of a winner's. Even if you're not winning scholarships, get back up and go right back to applying for them. This builds your endurance and resilience. The even greater achievement here is that you've already spoken over yourself and your circumstance to the point that when you come out of the hardship, you have so much trust in God that you know next time there's no way you can lose. This type of confidence and trust in Him erases the doubt. You have to start "calling down what is not as though it were", just as it is noted God does in **_Romans 4:17,_ _"As it is written: I have made you the father of many nations. He_** [Abraham] **_believed in God, who gives life to the dead and calls things into existence that do not exist."_** It's a mind game in which you're tricking your mind to really believe what you speak, and as a result it builds your confidence in God. I believe it's your confidence that God wants to see.

## Valerie Fomengia, Hampton University Class of 2010

I know it was God who got me each and every scholarship, each and every semester. In high school, I applied for 15-20 scholarships, but only received two. Between my financial aid package and my dad contributing to my college expenses, my freshman year was taken care of. The summer after my freshman year, however, I knew I was not going to have enough money to get me through sophomore year. I actually cried because I didn't know how I would come back to school. But I started doing three things: 1) Appling for a lot of scholarships; 2) Praying over each scholarship before mailing it off; and 3) Faithfully tithing with my work study money, my internship money, and even money that I would received from family members. That was when I started receiving the scholarships that I was applying for. I received one that same summer, another one in October (first semester of sophomore year), and two more during that second semester.

My entire mindset changed during the second semester of my sophomore year. I devoted 110% of my time to ministry. I was heavily involved in the Student Christian Association as a leader, spearheading and participating in many of its on-campus events. I gave a lot of my time to God and I consciously put Him first. That semester became the only semester during my college tenure in which I received all As, and even a few A-pluses. In that semester I also established a rapport with the Dean of my school, who offered me work study to work for him! God just worked it all out.

After my sophomore year, I continued to apply for scholarships, pray over each one, and tithe. But the summer before my junior year, I contemplated leaving Hampton because yet again it seemed as if there was no way I would be able to afford the cost of attendance that year. I made a decision on which community college back home in Maryland I was going to attend. I even called the company I had done my internship with for the previous two years to inquire if my attending a community college would affect my internship status for the upcoming summers, which I was told it would not. I anticipated receiving a scholarship from the department of my major but I knew it was highly unlikely that I would receive it in time to pay for tuition. To verify, I called my department secretary just before returning back to school in August and asked her when the scholarship would be disbursed. I heard the date and told her it would not be available in time for me to come back to Hampton. But then she responded, "Hold on." She looked through her records and said, "We can double the award and provide it in time to be applied to your student account." With that, I ended up receiving more than what I anticipated, earlier than when I anticipated receiving it! The amount covered the expenses for my entire junior year. On top of that, an opportunity to work for one of my professors presented itself in October. Because of the work ethic I displayed during my work study for the Dean, as well as the rapport we continued, he mentioned my name to my professor who was looking for a student to help him with one of his research studies. I knew nothing about this, nor did I ask, but I eagerly accepted the opportunity when it came. As an added benefit, the work study paid a stipend that was more than what work study students typically get paid.

After this point I continued to apply for scholarships, pray over each one, and tithe faithfully. All the scholarships I applied for, I received. Even one scholarship in particular that I had applied to every year but never received, I received it my senior year. In addition, it was a recurring scholarship so with me being in the Five-Year MBA Program and having to stay at Hampton for one more year past my senior year, the scholarship also applied to my graduate year.

It was when I really started trusting God and praying and putting Him first in my life that everything started working out. There is scholarship money out there. Reach out to your resources like the financial aid office and local organizations (i.e. church, Boys & Girls Clubs, alumni chapters, companies). Talk with the Dean of your school. Follow up with those resources each semester because new opportunities always pop up. Be persistent. My experiences taught me the importance of never giving up. Most importantly, pray your way through. Know that if God wants you to be at that college, then He's going to make it happen. Give thanks, give God praise, and bless somebody else.

> *"When he entered the house, the blind men approached him, and Jesus said to them, 'Do you believe that I can* ["can" is "am able to" in other versions] *do this?' 'Yes, Lord,' they answered Him. Then He touched their eyes, saying, 'Let it be done for you according to your faith!' And their eyes were opened." (Matthew 9:28-30)*

Notice, it was their **FAITH** that brought them the healing. Whether it is a healing for your body or scholarship money you need for college, your faith will spring forth your blessing.

# Resource Guide

Here's a list of resources that I compiled (in no particular order) for students looking to obtain college planning and scholarship information. I personally utilized, applied to and won scholarships from many of these resources. Feel free to peruse by the categorized topics. This list contains over 150 resources, but there are many more out there waiting to be found by YOU! Do you research, ask questions, remain diligent, and keep your faith.

## BOOKS

1. <u>2007-2009 African American Scholarship Guide for Students & Parents</u> by Dante Lee
2. <u>Black Excel African American Student's College Guide</u> by Isaac Black
3. <u>How to Go to College Almost for Free</u> by Ben Kaplan
4. <u>Paying for College Without Going Broke, 2012 Edition</u> by Princeton Review and Kalman Chany
5. <u>Scholarships, Grants and Prizes 2011</u> by Peterson's
6. <u>Scholarship Handbook 2012</u> by The College Board
7. <u>The Scholarship Book, 13th Edition: The Complete Guide to Private-Sector Scholarships, Fellowships, Grants, and Loans for the Undergraduate</u> by Daniel Cassidy
8. <u>The Ultimate Scholarship Book 2012: Billions of Dollars in Scholarships, Grants and Prizes</u> by Kelly Tanabe

*Amazon.com lists many similar books specifically geared towards minority students*

# WEBSITES

1.  **Adventures In Education**
    http://www.aie.org/
2.  **Bureau of Labor Statistics, Occupations Outlook Handbook**
    http://www.bls.gov/oco/
3.  **The Princeton Review, College Research**
    http://www.princetonreview.com/college-education.aspx
4.  **College Answer, Sallie Mae**
    http://www.collegeanswer.com/index.jsp
5.  **4BlackYouth**
    http://4blackyouth.com/Career.aspx

## *\*Federal Resources\*\**

6.  **Federal Work Study (FWS) Program**
    http://www2.ed.gov/programs/fws/index.html
7.  **Federal Pell Grant**
    http://www2.ed.gov/programs/fpg/index.html
8.  **U.S. Department of Education, State Higher Education Agencies**
    http://wdcrobcolp01.ed.gov/Programs/EROD/org_list.
    cfm?category_ID=SHE
9.  **Free Application for Federal Student Aid (FAFSA)**
    http://www.fafsa.ed.gov/
10. **Federal Student Aid**
    http://studentaid.ed.gov/PORTALSWebApp/students/
    english/f unding.jsp
11. **FinAid**
    http://www.finaid.org/otheraid/tax.phtml

## *\*General Scholarships & Scholarships for Minorities\*\**

12. **College Scholarships.org**
    www.collegescholarships.org
13. **StudentAid.com**
    www.studentaid.com
14. **College Board**
    www.collegeboard.com

15. **Fastweb**
    www.fastweb.com
16. **Scholarships Online**
    www.scholarshipsonline.org
17. **Scholarships.com**
    http://www.scholarships.com/main.aspx
18. **General Scholarships (database hosted by University of Miami)**
    http://www.miami.edu/admission/index.php/
    undergraduate_admission/costsandfinancialresources/
    scholarships/scholarship_database/general_scholarships
19. **Multicultural Student Scholarships (database hosted by University of Miami)**
    http://www.miami.edu/admission/index.php/
    undergraduate_admission/costsandfinancialresources/
    scholarships/scholarship_database/multicultural_student_
    scholarships
20. **Gates Millennium Scholars Program**
    http://www.gmsp.org/(hmrfvje1fdxdi0nwbrpmbd45)/
    default.aspx
21. **Ronald McDonald House Charities**
    http://rmhc.org/assets/RMHC-ScholarshipPDFs/
    RMHScholars2010-2011.pdf
22. **My College Options**
    https://www.mycollegeoptions.org/scholarship-search-by-
    ethnicity.aspx
23. **FinancialAidFinder**
    http://www.financialaidfinder.com/student-scholarship-
    search/
24. **National Merit Scholarship Corporation**
    www.nationalmerit.org
25. **Nationally Coveted College Scholarships, Graduate Fellowships & Postdoctoral Awards**
    http://scholarships.fatomei.com/
26. **Elks National Foundation**
    http://www.elks.org/enf/scholars/mvs.Cfm
27. **Burger King Scholars Program**
    http://www.haveityourwayfoundation.org/bksp_
    scholarship_eligibility.html
28. **Consumer Fraud Reporting Scholarship Lists**
    http://www.consumerfraudreporting.org/
    ScholarshipGrantList.php
29. **Scholarships and Grants**
    http://www.scholarshipsandgrants.us/

30. **FinAid Prestigious Scholarships and Fellowships**
    http://www.finaid.org/scholarships/prestigious.phtml
31. **FindTuition**
    http://www.findtuition.com/
32. **Coca-Cola Scholars Program**
    https://www.coca-colascholars.org/page.aspx?pid=388
33. **Ayn Rand Novels, Essay Contests**
    http://aynrandnovels.com/essay-contests.html
34. **U.S. Air Force ROTC Scholarships**
    http://afrotc.com/scholarships/
35. **Army ROTC Scholarships**
    http://www.goarmy.com/rotc/scholarships.html
36. **Navy ROTC Program**
    http://www.nrotc.navy.mil/program_info.aspx
37. **Marine Officer NROTC Program**
    http://officer.marines.com/marine/making_marine_officers/
    commissioning_programs/nrotc
38. **SuperCollege**
    http://www.supercollege.com/
39. **Peterson's College Search**
    http://www.petersons.com/college-search/scholarship-search.aspx
40. **Edison Scholars Program**
    http://sms.scholarshipamerica.org/edison/index.html
41. **Civil Rights Defense Fund**
    http://www.nradefensefund.org/contests-scholarships.aspx
42. **DegreeDirectory**
    http://degreedirectory.org/pages/Online_Associates_
    Degree_Scholarship.html
43. **National Association of Students Financial Aid Administrators**
    http://www.nasfaa.org/Search.aspx?searchtext=scholarship
44. **American Fire Sprinkler Association Scholarship Program**
    http://www.afsascholarship.org/
45. **Davidson Fellows Scholarships**
    http://www.davidsongifted.org/Fellows/
46. **National Society of High School Scholarships**
    http://www.nshss.org/scholarships/
47. **American Political Science Association, Minority Scholar Resources**
    http://www.apsanet.org/PS/grants/aspen3.cfm
48. **Horatio Alger Association of Distinguished Americans,**
    **Scholarship Programs**
    http://www.horatioalgerorg/scholarships
49. **Every Chance Every Texan, Scholarships and Other Financial Aid**
    http://www.window.state.tx.us/scholars/aid/faidalpha.html

50. **Recession Relief Scholarship**
    http://www.straightforwardmedia.com/debt/debt—
    scholarship.html
51. **A Better Chance**
    http://www.abetterchance.org/abetterchance.
    aspx?pgID=1098
52. **Miss America, Scholarship Directory**
    http://www.missamerica.org/scholarships/scholarship—
    directory.aspx
53. **FinAid, Scholarships for Volunteering and Community Service**
    http://www.finaid.org/scholarships/service.phtml
54. **LAGRANT Foundation**
    http://www.lagrantfoundation.org/Scholarship%20Program
55. **Alliance for Young Artists and Writers**
    http://www.artandwriting.org/Scholarships
56. **Collegiate Inventors Competition**
    http://www.invent.org/collegiate/
57. **Research Associateship Programs**
    http://sites.nationalacademies.org/pga/rap/
58. **4BlackYouth**
    http://4blackyouth.com/scholarships.aspx?id=minority
59. **Be An Actuary**
    http://www.beanactuary.org/study/?fa=scholarship
60. **INROADS**
    http://www.inroads.org/search/node/scholarship
61. **Oxford and the Rhodes Scholarships**
    http://www.rhodesscholar.org/applying-for-the-scholarship/
    oxford-the-rhodes-scholarships/

## ** Scholarships for African Americans **

62. **NAACP**
    www.naacp.org/scholarship
63. **Black Excel Scholarship Gateway**
    http://www.blackexcel.org/link4.htm
64. **The Sallie Mae Fund, Black College Dollars**
    www.salliemae/black student dollars
65. **BlackStudents**
    http://blackstudents.blacknews.com/
66. **Black News.com, Black Scholarships and Grants**
    http://www.blacknews.com/directory/black_african_
    american_ scholarships.shtml

67. **The Jackie Robinson Foundation**
    http://www.jackierobinson.org/
68. **Scholarships.com, African American Scholarships**
    http://www.scholarships.com/financial-aid/college-
    scholarships/scholarships-by-type/minority—scholarships/
    african-american-scholarships/
69. **United Negro College Fund**
    www.uncf.org
70. **Black/African Descent Student Scholarships (database hosted by University of Miami)**
    http://www.miami.edu/admission/index.php/
    undergraduate_admission/costsandfinancialresources/
    scholarships/scholarship_database/black_african_descent
    _student_scholarships
71. **FinAid, Minority Students**
    http://www.finaid.org/otheraid/minority.phtml
72. **Ron Brown Scholar Program**
    http://www.ronbrown.org/
73. **Thurgood Marshall College Fund**
    http://www.thurgoodmarshallfund.org/
74. **Online Education Database, African American College Scholarships**
    http://oedb.org/scholarship/african-american
75. **American Institute of CPAs**
    http://www.aicpa.org/_catalogs/masterpage/Search.aspx?S=
    scholarship
76. **College Scholarships, African American College Grants**
    http://www.collegescholarships.org/grants/african—american.htm
77. **Sachs Foundation**
    http://www.sachsfoundation.org/
78. **Boeing**
    http://www.boeing.com/educationrelations/
79. **Xerox**
    http://www.xeroxstudentcareers.com/why-xerox/scholarship. aspx

## ** *Scholarships for Hispanic Americans* **

80. **Adelante U.S. Education Leadership Fund**
    http://www.adelantefund.org/adelante/Scholarships1.asp?
    SnID=278304716
81. **The National Council of La Raza's (NCLR) Lideres Initiative**
    http://lideres.nclr.org/section/opportunities/bestbuyscholarship1

82. **Hispanic Association of Colleges and Universities**
    http://www.hacu.net/hacu/Scholarships.asp
83. **Hispanic College Fund**
    http://hispanicfund.org/programs/college/scholarships
84. **Fastweb, Scholarships for Hispanic and Latino Students**
    http://www.fastweb.com/college-scholarships/articles/19-
    scholarships-for-hispanic-and-latino-students
85. **Hispanic Scholarship Fund**
    http://www.hsf.net/innercontent.aspx?id=34
86. **Chicana/Latina Foundation Scholarship Program**
    http://www.chicanalatina.org/scholarship.html
87. **Congressional Hispanic Caucus Institute (CHCI)**
    http://www.chci.org/scholarships/
88. **Latino College Dollars**
    http://www.latinocollegedollars.org/directory.htm
89. **Online Education Database, Hispanic College Scholarships**
    http://oedb.org/scholarship/hispanic
90. **Scholarship Hispanic**
    http://www.scholarshiphispanic.com/
91. **Hispanic/Latino Student Scholarships (database hosted by University of Miami)**
    http://www.miami.edu/admission/index.php/undergraduate
    _admission/costsandfinancialresources/scholarships/
    scholarship_database/hispanic_latino_student_scholarships
92. **Scholarships.com, Hispanic Scholarships**
    http://www.scholarships.com/financial-aid/college—
    scholarships/scholarships-by-type/minority-scholarships/
    hispanic-scholarships/


**_** Scholarships for American Indian/Alaskan Natives **_**


93. **Native American/American Indian Student Scholarships (database hosted by University of Miami)**
    http://www.miami.edu/admission/index.php/
    undergraduate_admission/costsandfinancialresources/
    scholarships/scholarship_database/native_american_
    american_indian_student_scholarships
94. **Alaska Native Tribal Health Consortium**
    http://www.collegefund.org/students_and_alumni/content/
    scholarships
95. **American Indian Education Program**
    http://indianeducation.spps.org/Scholarship_Information.html

96. **FinAid, Financial Aid for Native American Students**
http://www.finaid.org/otheraid/natamind.phtml
97. **Scholarships.com, American Indian (Native American) Scholarships**
http://www.scholarships.com/financial-aid/college—scholarships/scholarships-by-type/minority—scholarships/american-indian-native-american-scholarships/
98. **National Indian Law Library**
http://www.narf.org/nill/resources/scholarships.htm
99. **Association on American Indian Affairs**
http://www.indian-affairs.org/scholarships/aaia_scholarships. htm
100. **American Indian Graduate Center**
http://www.aigc.com/

## ** *Scholarships for Asian-American/ Pacific Islander Americans* **

101. **College Scholarships, Asian American Scholarships**
http://www.collegescholarships.org/scholarships/asian.htm
102. **Asian Student Scholarships (database hosted by University of Miami)**
http://www.miami.edu/admission/index.php/undergraduate_a dmission/costsandfinancialresources/scholarships/scholarship _database/asian_student_scholarships
103. **Asian American Journalists Association**
http://www.aaja.org/category/programs/college/
104. **U.S. Pan Asian American Chamber of Commerce Education Foundation**
http://celebrasianconference.com/about-celebrasian/scholarships/overview/
105. **Asian & Pacific Islander American Scholarship Fund**
http://www.apiasf.org/
106. **Asian American Giving**
http://www.asianamericangiving.com/grantsawards scholarships/
107. **OCA**
http://www.ocanational.org/index.php?option=com_content&t ask=view&id=59&Itemid=
108. **Scholarships.com, Asian Scholarships**
http://www.scholarships.com/financial-aid/college—scholarships/scholarships-by-type/minority—scholarships/asian-scholarships/

## ** Scholarships for Arab Americans **

109. **Arab American Institute**
     http://www.aaiusa.org/pages/scholarships/
110. **American-Arab Anti-Discrimination Committee**
     http://www.adc.org/education/arab-american-scholarships/
111. **Lebanese American Heritage Club**
     http://www.lahc.org/scholarship1
112. **USEG Tours**
     http://www.usegtours.com/aljamiat_aid.htm
113. **American Islamic Congress**
     http://www.hamsaweb.org/essay/

## ** Scholarships for Women **

114. **FinAid, Financial Aid for Female Students**
     http://www.finaid.org/otheraid/female.phtml
115. **Scholarships for Women (database hosted by University of Miami)**
     http://www.miami.edu/admission/index.php/
     undergraduate_a dmission/costsandfinancialresources/
     scholarships/scholarship _database/scholarships_for_women
116. **Jeannette Rankin Women's Scholarship Fund**
     http://www.rankinfoundation.org/
117. **New York Women in Communications Foundation**
     http://www.nywici.org/foundation/scholarships
118. **The Google Anita Borg Memorial Scholarship**
     http://www.google.com/anitaborg/
119. **American Association of University Women**
     http://www.aauw.org/learn/awards/index.cfm
120. **Scholarships.com, Scholarships for Women**
     http://www.scholarships.com/financial-aid/college—
     scholarships/scholarships-by-type/scholarships-for-women/

## ** Scholarships for Single Mothers/Single Parents **

121. **EducationGrant**
     http://www.educationgrant.com/scholarships/scholarships—
     for-single-mothers/

122. **Scholarships.com, College Scholarships and Grants for Single Mothers**
http://www.scholarships.com/financial-aid/college—
scholarships/scholarships-by-type/college-scholarships-and—
grants-for-single-mothers/
123. **About.com, State-by-State List of Scholarships for Single Parents**
http://singleparents.about.com/od/adulteducation/a/
scholarships_us.htm \

## ** *Scholarships for Orphans* **

124. **Foster Care to Success**
http://www.fc2success.org/programs/scholarships-and—grants/
125. **Foresters**
http://www.foresters.com/us-en/membership/grants—
scholarships/pages/default.aspx
126. **Ohio War Orphans Scholarship**
http://regents.ohio.gov/sgs/war_orphans/

## ** *Scholarships by Military Association* **

127. **FinAid, Financial Aid for Veterans and their Dependents**
http://www.finaid.org/military/veterans.phtml

128. **Military Scholarships (database hosted by University of Miami)**
http://www.miami.edu/admission/index.php/
undergraduate_a dmission/costsandfinancialresources/
scholarships/scholarship _database/military_scholarships

129. **Fisher House Foundation**
http://www.militaryscholar.org/

130. **U.S. Air Force ROTC**
http://afrotc.com/scholarships/

131. **Marine Corps Scholarship Foundation**
http://www.marine-scholars.org/

132. **Scholarships.com, Virginia War Orphans Education Program**
http://www.scholarships.com/financial-aid/college—
scholarships/scholarships-by-state/virginia—scholarships/
virginia-war-orphans-education-program/

133. **Armed Forces Communications and Electronics Association (AFCEA) Educational Foundation**
     http://www.afcea.org/education/scholarships/undergradu ate/DisabledVeteranScholarship.asp

## ** Scholarships Based on Your September 11th Association **

134. **Families of Freedom Scholarship Fund**
     http://www.familiesoffreedom.org/
135. **Scholarships4Students, 9-11 Scholarships**
     http://www.scholarships4students.com/9-11_scholarships. htm
136. **British Council, UK 9/11 Scholarship Funds**
     http://www.britishcouncil.org/911scholarships.htm

## ** Scholarships Based on Your Unique Traits **

137. **FinAid, Cancer Scholarships**
     http://www.finaid.org/scholarships/cancer.phtml
138. **Proyecto Vision**
     http://www.proyectovision.net/english/opportunities/ scholars hips.html
139. **Scholarships for Students with Disabilities (database hosted by University of Miami)**
     http://www.miami.edu/admission/index.php/ undergraduate_a dmission/costsandfinancialresources/ scholarships/scholarship _database/scholarships_for_ students_with_disabilities
140. **National Federation of the Blind**
     http://www.nfb.org/scholarship-program
141. **Disabled World**
     http://www.disabled-world.com/disability/education/ scholarships/
142. **UCB Family Epilepsy Scholarship Program**
     http://www.ucbepilepsyscholarship.com/
143. **Autism Society**
     http://www.autism-society.org/about-us/awards-scholarships/
144. **The Roothbert Fund**
     http://www.roothbertfund.org/scholarships.php

## ** Scholarships by College/Location **

145. **Guaranteed Scholarships**
     http://www.guaranteed-scholarships.com/
146. **MyCollegeOptions**
     https://www.mycollegeoptions.org/scholarship-search-by—
     location.aspx

## ** Scholarships by Major **

147. **CollegeScholarships.org, Discovery Subject Specific Scholarships**
     http://www.collegescholarships.org/scholarships/subject—
     specific.htm
148. **MyCollegeOptions**
     https://www.mycollegeoptions.org/scholarship-search-by—
     ethnicity.aspx
149. **Business Student Scholarships (database hosted by University of Miami)**
     http://www.miami.edu/admission/index.php/undergradu
     ate_admission/costsandfinancialresources/scholarships/
     scholarship_database/business_student_scholarships
150. **Scholarships.com, Scholarships by Major**
     http://www.scholarships.com/financial-aid/college—
     scholarships/scholarships-by-major/

## ** Scholarships for Graduate Students **

151. **Graduate Scholarships, Fellowships and Loans (database hosted by Michigan State University)**
     http://staff.lib.msu.edu/harris23/grants/3gradinf.htm
152. **Graduate Scholarships (database hosted by University of Miami)**
     http://www.miami.edu/index.php/office_of_financial_
     assistance/g/g_programs/g_scholarships/graduate_
     scholarship_database

## ** Scholarships for STEM Majors **

153. **Astronaut Scholarship Foundation**
     http://www.astronautscholarship.org/

154. **Engineering Education Service Center**
    http://www.engineeringedu.com/scholars.html
155. **Science and Engineering Student Scholarships (database hosted by University of Miami)**
    http://www.miami.edu/admission/index.php/undergradu ate_admission/costsandfinancialresources/scholarships/ sc holarship_database/science_engineering_student_ scholarships
156. **National Hydropower Association (NHA), Past Presidents' Legacy Scholarship**
    http://hydro.org/about-nha/awards/past-presidents%E2% 80%99-legacy-scholarship/
157. **American Chemical Society**
    http://portal.acs.org/portal/acs/corg/content?_nfpb=true&_ pa geLabel=PP_TRANSITIONMAIN&node_id=1234&use_ sec=false& sec_url_var=region1&__uuid=a172f9a4-2784- 4318-9d97—f40e4d61f235

## ** *Scholarships to Study Abroad* **

158. **IES Abroad**
    https://www.iesabroad.org/IES/Scholarships_and_Aid/ financialAid.html
159. **SIT Study Abroad**
    http://www.sit.edu/studyabroad/scholarships.htm
160. **Institute Of International Education, Benjamin A. Gilman International Scholarship**
    http://www.iie.org/en/Programs/Gilman-Scholarship— Program/About-the-Program

# Acknowledgments

*From the bottom of my heart, I would like to thank the following people for contributing their experiences, thoughts, insight, ideas and resources to this book:*

*Amanda McLean, my dear cousin. It pays to have a schoolteacher in the family! Thank you for reviewing the language in this book with eagle eyes. More so, thank you for your dedication and commitment in helping me to release it.*

*Andy McLean, my wonderful father. Thank you for being my eyes and ears as I prepared myself to publish this book. Thank you for understanding my vision for this book and for giving me your full support on it. Thank you for the financial support and sacrifices you made while I attended college. I love you eternally.*

*Chris McLean, my brother and new college graduate. I appreciate the concerns and frustrations regarding scholarships that you expressed to me. I was able to address them within the book. I hope future college students with the same frustrations will be able to read my book and know that there is more than enough scholarship money out there to easily attain. Thank you.*

*Courtney Mitchell, DeQuan Smith, Lorreanne Webley, and Valerie Fomengia, dear friends of mine. I love you for the support and assistance you provided me with by sharing your personal experiences with scholarships.*

*Dr. Ruby Beale and Dr. Ziette Hayes, School of Business Professors at Hampton University and mentors of mine. Thank you for cheering me on as God continued to bless me with scholarships. I always tried to* represent the School as best as I could, always to find that you two were in the background supporting me. Thank you.

Heather Carreiro, my lovely coworker. God places certain people in your life at certain points to help you on your journey in Him. Thank you for being in a position to help me understand the publishing process and to willingly provide me with all of the advice and insight that your previous work experiences taught you.

Kris McLean, my teacher, my inspiration, my prayer warrior, my mother. Many more titles, but we'll leave it at that. Thank you for instilling God's Word and prayer in my life, for it was the foundation of my scholarship faith. Thank you for following up on scholarships for me, reminding me of my deadlines, and calling my financial aid office countless times to get things "straightened." You supported me in more ways than one as I embarked on this writing journey. Thank you for the love, guidance and support.

Kyle McLean, my baby brother and current high school student. You are my inspiration. I hope you and all other current high school students will benefit from the words in this book. I love you.

Lakesha Luma, an educator and the daughter of Mrs. Joyce Malette. Thank you for the talking points you've added to my book in regards to where students can look for scholarships. You were more help to me than you realize!

Melody and Robert Ellis, my dear Aunt and Uncle. Thank you for the edits and spiritual support you provided during the final stages of creating this book.

Mr. David Mitnick, my high school Guidance Counselor. I certainly would not be where I am today, financially, without your support. I received about $20,000 in scholarships for my first year of college because of your work ethic and your guidance in helping me to secure all of it. You also allowed me to interview you for much of commentary added to this book. You are truly a blessing, and I thank you.

*Mr. William Smith, Scholarship Coordinator of Hampton University. You have been a necessary scholarship resource since before I stepped on campus as a freshman. My mother called you on numerous occasions, asking about my scholarships. I suppose you did not know her then, but you've come to know me throughout my stay at Hampton as I frequented your office to inquire about scholarships. Thank you for your passion to get the word out to students about all of this free money. Thank you for the plethora of advice you allowed me to add to this book.*

*Mrs. Malette, a loving mother and dear friend of mine. You provided me with great advice and resources when I came to you about publishing a book based on my scholarships winnings, not to mention that you created a scholarship in memory of your daughter of which I was a recipient my senior year of high school. Thank you for your love and support.*

*Mrs. Robin Foreman, Director of the Hampton Roads Community Foundation. You provided me with many of the talking points used throughout this book on what students should do to avail themselves to scholarship money. Thank you for the interview.*

*Nicole Ellis, a poet and peer. You gave me the motivation I needed to walk in full confidence to publish this book. You told me about how much this book would be needed for parents and students. An author yourself, you gave me a lot of great advice about publishing. Thank you.*

*Pastor Brian Bellamy, my Pastor and friend. Your personal experiences with scholarships were great additions to the book. Thank you for the spiritual guidance you also provided to make this book not only a guide but also an evangelistic tool.*

**Prayer. Word. Worship. Faith.**

# Notes

1.  "Trends in College Pricing 2011," College Board Advocacy & Policy Center. 2011 <http://trends.collegeboard.org/downloads/College_Pricing_2011.pdf>.
2.  *Vision & Mission,* The Executive Leadership Council. 2011. <http://www.elcinfo.com/mission.php>.
3.  *Higher Education Ministry, 2012-2013 Scholarship Program, Available Scholarships,* Cascade United Methodist Church. 2012. <http://www.cascadeumc.info//scholarship_award_list.asp>.
4.  *Jesse Brown Scholarships,* Disabled American Veterans. 2012. <http://www.dav.org/volunteers/Scholarship.aspx>.
5.  "Kohl's Cares® Scholarship Program." Kohl's Foundation. 2012. <http://www.kohlscorporation.com/communityrelations/scholarship/index.asp>.
6.  *SCAD Challenge Scholarship Competition,* The Savannah College of Art and Design. 2011. <http://www.scad.edu/scadchallenge/>.
7.  "Scholarships." The San Diego Foundation 2012. <http://www.sdfoundation.org/GrantsScholarships/Scholarships.aspx>.
8.  "Trends in College Pricing 2011." College Board Advocacy & Policy Center. 2011. <http://www.trends.collegeboard.org/downloads/College_Pricing_2011.pdf>.
9.  "The Hidden Costs of College and How to Budget for Them," Seventeen Magazine. 2011. <http://www.seventeen.com/college/advice>.
10. "Average Intern Salaries," SimplyHired.com. 2011. < http://www.simplyhired.com/a/salary/search/q-intern>.
11. "What It Costs to Go to College," CollegeBoard.com. 2011. <http://www.collegeboard.com/student/pay/add-it-up/4494.html>.
12. Lazarony, Lucy. "College for Half-Price," BankRate.com. Jan. 8, 2008. <http://articles.moneycentral.msn.com/CollegeAndFamily/CutCollegeCosts/CollegeForHalfPrice.aspx>.
13. "Women, Minorities, and Persons with Disabilities in Science and Engineering: 2011," National Science Foundation. 2011. <http://www.nsf.gov/statistics/wmpd/pdf/nsf11309.pdf>.
14. "Uncovering the Truth About and Protecting Yourself from Scholarship Scams," GoCollege.com. 2011. <http://www.gocollege.com/financial-aid/scholarships/apply/scholarship-scams.html>.

[15]  "Strengthening Head Start: What Evidence Shows," U.S. Department of Health and Human Services. <http://aspe.hhs.gov/hsp/strengthenheadstart03/report.htm#IVA>.

[16]  "What is a 529 Plan?" Savingforcollege.com. 2011. <http://www.savingforcollege.com/intro_to_529s/what-is-a-529-plan.php>.

[17]  *Gerber Life College Plan,* Gerberlife.com. 2011. <https://www.gerberlife.com/gl/view/guide_products/college/index.jsp>.

[18]  *Salvation Page,* Friendship Baptist Church. 2012. <http://www.friendshipmbc.net/salvation_page.html>.